The **Unshackled Organization**

The **Unshackled**

Organization

**FACING THE CHALLENGE OF
UNPREDICTABILITY THROUGH
SPONTANEOUS REORGANIZATION**

BY JEFFREY GOLDSTEIN

PUBLISHER'S MESSAGE BY NORMAN BODEK

PRODUCTIVITY PRESS
PORTLAND, OREGON

Productivity Press
P.O. Box 13390
Portland OR 97213-0390
United States of America
Telephone: 503-235-0600
Telefax: 503-235-0909

ISBN: 1-56327-048-X

Cover and book design by Bill Stanton
Interior layout and typesetting by Frank Loose Design
Printed and bound by Maple-Vail Book Manufacturing Group
in the United States of America

Library of Congress Cataloging-in-Publication Data:

Goldstein, Jeffrey, 1949-
      The unshackled organization : facing the challenge of unpredictability through spontaneous reorganization / by Jeffrey Goldstein.
        p. cm.
      Includes bibliographical references and index.
      ISBN 1-56327-048-X
        1. Organizational change. 2. Corporate culture. 3. Corporate reorganizations.
I. Title.
HD58.8.G627 1994
302.3'5—dc20   94-983
                                                  CIP

98 97 96 95 94 10 9 8 7 6 5 4 3 2

CONTENTS

PUBLISHER'S MESSAGE

*I*n a time when managers are scrambling to find methods to maneuver through the madness of a completely unpredictable business environment, Jeffrey Goldstein's answers are surprising, challenging, and sometimes controversial. But when applied, they reveal the key to highly refined organization functioning. In *The Unshackled Organization,* consultant and management professor Jeffrey Goldstein examines new territory with his exploration into how change happens within an organization.

Utilizing leading-edge scientific and social theories about change, Goldstein shows that only through *self-organization* can natural, lasting change occur. With compelling examples and innovative theories, Goldstein challenges the change agent's traditional role of managing resistance, creating consensus, and planning and controlling a change process. All of these concepts must be abandoned if we are to understand how change actually takes place, and if we are to become effective leaders.

The theory behind self-organization comes from the idea of allowing and even amplifying unpredictable fluctuation and differences rather than abolishing or controlling them. In other words: "Don't fight it!" Change imposed through hierarchical control rarely matches the long-term needs of the organization and often is not accepted with open arms by employees. Internal problems may be the source of new, more effective structures trying to develop to match the changing demands being placed on the organization. When such problems are ignored or managers attempt to eliminate them with short-term solutions, deeper problems may develop whose source may be more difficult to understand and solve. By stimulating change from within the organization, however, managers may witness the natural emergence of long-lasting, structural improvements, and the development of an increasingly effective team of people.

Goldstein explores the aspects of chaos theory and system dynamics that can be applied meaningfully to organization change: non-linearity versus linearity, far-from-equilibrium conditions versus shifting states of equilibrium, feedback, attractors versus resistance, self-organization, system boundaries, and unpredictability. He walks the reader through the application of these concepts as management methods for initiating self-organization in teams and organization settings. The book provides exercises and examples of the use of many methods where equilibrium is challenged effectively to cause teams to create better modes of communication, more appropriate policies, enhanced operations, increased productivity, and higher morale. Some of the companies examined have been given hypothetical names to protect their privacy, but all the examples used are real and the changes described that resulted from self-organization have been lasting.

It is a great pleasure for us at Productivity Press to publish this innovative book on organization change. We wish to express our thanks to all who participated in creating this fine book: Karen Jones, managing editor, for meeting impossible deadlines and extending them with good grace on occasion; Jennifer Albert, editorial assistant, for updating revisions of the manuscript; Catchword, Inc. for indexing; Bill Stanton, production manager, for the beautiful cover and text design; Susan Swanson, production assistant, for keeping the production process on track; Frank Loose for typesetting and layout; and Hannah Bonner, cartoonist extraordinaire, for her insight and creativity.

Norman Bodek, Publisher
Diane Asay, Acquisitions Editor

PREFACE

his book presents a practical approach to organizational change derived from state-of-the-art scientific research into how systems change. As a result, it relies on scientific terminology that may be unfamiliar to many readers. I want to reassure the reader that all of these new terms and concepts are fully explained for the non-scientist, and, furthermore, that there is neither a math nor a science prerequisite for reading this book! In fact, the book does not contain even one equation!

Since the scientific research at the basis of the new model was conducted on physical systems, a translation needs to take place from physical systems to the social system of a modern organization. This is one of the tasks of the book: to decipher these exciting scientific discoveries so they are applicable in the arena of our businesses and institutions.

The reason for turning to mathematics and the sciences for understanding organizational change rests in the truly tremendous leaps forward that have taken place over the past thirty years in understanding system change. Unfortunately, organizational practice has not only not yet caught up with these startling insights, to a large extent it is still relying on models of system change established in the nineteenth century. Only now, as we near the end of the century, are we beginning to bring organizational thinking even into the twentieth century.

The new model of organizational change is meant to be a pragmatic guide for managers, executives, consultants, and other change agents. Consequently, the elements of the new approach are illustrated by real world examples about diverse types of organizational change drawn from a variety of organizations.

The organizations represented are large, small and mid-range, profit and not-for-profit, private and public. All of these examples are real situations. However, to protect the anonymity of those involved in the changes described, many of the change situations have been camouflaged in name, even type of industry. These changes are indicated by quotation marks around the names of the organizations: "..."

Sometimes the differences between the new model and the traditional one are subtle; many times they are not. From the perspective of the new model, the traditional approach is seen as a limiting case of the more general new model. Accordingly, it is my claim that when an organizational change project is successful, its dynamics can be better understood in terms of the new model than the traditional one. Moreover, the new model can pinpoint the reasons why a change intervention that should have been successful wasn't.

Even though this book presents an approach to organizational change which is thoroughly modern, in many ways these new insights are simply a contemporary rediscovery of ancient wisdom concerning the process of change. Nowhere has this ancient wisdom on change been more far-reaching or prescient than in ancient China, particularly in the great Chinese classic, *I Ching,* or *Book of Changes.* Therefore, each chapter opens with a quote from the *I Ching,* from the classic text of Taoism, the *Tao te Ching,* or from a great sage such as Chuang Tzu. The West still has quite a lot of work to do to catch up with those ancient sages.

Jeffrey Goldstein

Acknowledgments

*O*ver the past several years, I have had the good fortune of many stimulating and challenging conversations, and many of the ideas discussed during these conversations have found their way into this book. In addition, this book contains many examples of change from a variety of organizations. For either being great "conversation-mates" or for providing me with appropriate examples, I am indebted to the following consultants, executives, managers, professors, and other "change agents":

Fred Abraham	Bracha Klein
Kevin Dooley	Lisa Marshall
Ann Drissell	Uri Merry
Carol Cryer	Rose Redding Mersky
Robert Ebers	Mark Michaels
Glenda Eoyang	Dick Nodell
Sally Goerner	Tom Shinnick
Steve Guastello	Larry Solow
Larry Hirschhorn	Maureen Sullivan
Wally Hlavac	Meg Wheatley
Nan Kilkeary	Brenda Zimmerman

Mark Michaels, president of People Technologies, and entrepreneur par excellence, also deserves special thanks. Through his efforts in creating *The Chaos Network Newsletter,* the Chaos Network On-line Computer Conference (through MetaNet), and the Annual Conferences, he has established an exciting, state-of-the-art forum for the application of the new sciences of chaos and nonlinear complex systems theory to social systems.

In addition, I would like to thank Diane Asay, my main editor at Productivity Press, who after listening to a presentation of mine several years ago thought there was a potential book among all those ideas and encouraged me to write it. Thank you also, Diane, for your nonlinear intuitions that helped guide me in the writing of this book.

I also want to thank Jennifer Albert, Julie Zinkus, and the other editors at Productivity Press for their insights concerning how I could clarify various sections of this book.

Many thanks to Hannah Bonner for her wonderful cartoons. I chuckle every time I read them.

> *We are caught in an inescapable network of mutuality, tied*
> *in a single garment of destiny. Whatever affects one directly,*
> *affects all indirectly.*
> —MARTIN LUTHER KING, JR.

1

NEW WINE SKINS

The image of the turning point...
The movement is natural, arising spontaneously.
The old is discarded and the new is introduced...
Therefore it is not necessary to hasten anything artificially.
—I CHING (HEXAGRAM 24 WITH COMMENTARY BY RICHARD WILHELM)

Our businesses and institutions are finally facing a difficult but undeniable truth: What worked in the past is no longer adequate for creating the future. A new future requires a new vision, and this new vision can bring about significant change only when it becomes embodied in new organizational practices. Deeply rooted change, though, is rarely an easy matter. There is an old Biblical saying that new wine cannot be stored in old wine skins or it will go sour. The times demand a fundamentally new approach for changing organizations, new wine skins for new wine.

Fortunately, a new approach is now at hand through a profound scientific revolution concerning how systems change. New research and theories demonstrate that under the right set of circumstances, systems can exhibit *self-organization*, a spontaneous and radical transformation in the structure and functioning of a system. Self-organization provides a powerful new model for guiding organizational change that surpasses the hierarchically controlled and resistance-busting strategies of the past.

Self-organization isn't offering a fast and painless way to transform organizations. If the old is really giving way to the new, struggle and difficulty signal that deep-rooted change is actually taking place. Consider the profound, natural passage of adolescence as a child slowly becomes an adult. There is the actual physical pain of growth, the inner

1

churning of new sensations and desires, and the anxiety accompanying the collapse of old childhood boundaries. These are signs that significant inner transformation is at work. Pain, churning, and discomfort may also accompany organizational change. Certainly many things will have to be done differently.

THE ALCHEMY OF SELF-ORGANIZATION

Consider this example of a difficult passage of self-organizing change at "PharmChem," a chemical specialty manufacturing firm in the Midwest. Several years ago, one of "PharmChem's" owners realized that its cumbersome bureaucracy inhibited rapid interactions inside the company, as well as between the company and its customers. As a result, the management pyramid was flattened and the company was restructured into six functionally linked groups.

A certain amount of anxiety accompanied this change. For example, at one of the meetings where the new structure was discussed, an employee blurted out: "You can't just impose this new structure and leave. You have not given us the tools or skills to pull this off. You've left us out in the wilderness!"

The owner responded that he didn't have the answers, but he could offer a few questions that the groups needed to address.

- Who shall lead each group?

- Who is willing to participate in the team-generated vision, mission, and purpose? Is vision different from the purpose? Is purpose different than the mission? How does the group's mission fit in with the mission of the company?

- What are the undiscussable issues concerning interpersonal conflict in the groups, and is anyone now willing to discuss them?

The owner didn't stay to answer these questions, for they would have been his answers and not theirs, but he did indicate that he would act as a consultant if they came to him for help.

These difficult questions had a churning effect on the groups, unearthing and challenging deeply rooted operating assumptions. Moreover, now members of the groups had only their internal resources to turn to, whereas in the past, someone higher up in the organization made the crucial determinations. Self-organization demands that a system draw upon its own resources, not the hierarchy's, in order to meet the challenges that face it. This was not laissez-faire leadership. Instead, there was much struggle and difficulty as "PharmChem" entered a dark passage with an uncertain outcome. One thing definitely occurred, however. The new functional groups were challenged in a way insured to bring out the capacity of a system to transform itself.

This inner organizational transformation is analogous to the processes of ancient alchemy in which chemical compounds would be challenged by various procedures in order to bring out their hidden essence. Because this essence was thought to be locked up inside each of the compounds, the skill of alchemy consisted of knowing the right means for challenging, and thereby facilitating inner transformation, in each of the compounds. Like alchemy, self-organization is a process of transformation whereby the inner potentials for change that are locked up in the organization are unleashed and actualized by the right kind of challenge.

Although the changes required by our organizations are often both vast and drastic, it does not necessarily follow that the kinds of challenges needed for self-organization also need to be vast and drastic.

CHALLENGING THE BOSS AT "CARVILLE GENERAL HOSPITAL"

"Carville General Hospital" is a 500-bed urban medical center in a city of about one million. "Carville General" had participated in a cost survey comparing it with similar hospitals in terms of size, case mix, and cost structure. Because it didn't fare too well in this survey, the Board of Trustees set overall cost reduction targets. The new CEO wanted the cost-cutting effort to dovetail with a new Total Quality Management program.

The project started with the formation of three initial project teams: a senior management team; an ancillary resource allocation team; and a supply team. A retreat was designed where the new teams could develop their team charters to consist of member roles and responsibilities as well as ground rules for meetings.

In the supply team, the necessity for starting meetings on time became a hot topic for two reasons. First, because being on the supply team was an extra duty in addition to their regular organizational responsibilities, the members wanted to insure that the time spent in the meetings was used as efficiently as possible. Second, during the previous authoritarian regime, top-management meetings rarely started on time, with the result that lower level managers would be merely waiting around until the senior managers showed up. This habitual tardiness even continued with the new CEO, who, despite his talk about a new direction and a new culture, didn't arrive at his own meetings on time.

The supply team's requirement of starting meetings on time penetrated the senior management team through a senior manager who was also a member of the supply team. This executive persuaded the senior management team to adopt the rule of starting on time, using the same rationale as the supply team had.

However, the senior management team was plagued by problems from the very beginning. Their team was the least receptive to the consultant's role in managing the process of reaching consensus on the team charter. They had an incomplete charter, their ground rules were not clearly defined or accepted, and the team meetings were characterized by much tangential discussion and lack of listening to each other.

The CEO's style in running the team meetings was also a roadblock. He would end his comments with the authoritarian sounding, "This is what we are going to do, right?" However, the new team charter contained a provision allowing the team members to impeach the team leader if consensus was reached. Eventually, the CEO's violation of the ground rule of coming to the meetings on time—plus the fact that the senior management team was not getting anywhere, whereas the other teams were prospering—prompted the senior managers to impeach the CEO as team leader. Their empowerment happened spontaneously and could not have resulted from the contradictory imposition of a participative culture on them. This self-organized event continued to ripple throughout the organization.

The impeachment of the CEO was possible because it was built into the team charter that the group members themselves had developed. One of the consultant's roles at the end of every meeting was to bring to the group's attention whether they had violated the rules of the team charter. Indeed, if this rule had been promulgated in the beginning of the program as a management mandate concerning all future meetings in the medical center, it most likely would not have had the self-organizing effect it did.

It should be pointed out that the impeachment was not an easy thing to do, and was certainly not anticipated at the beginning of the change project. After all, the CEO was the boss! Who knew what would take place next? If a challenge is really to prompt self-organization, a certain amount of churning must be expected along with a healthy dose of unpredictability.

DISCREPANCIES BETWEEN MODEL AND PRACTICE

As an organizational researcher as well as consultant, I am involved with both the practical and theoretical nature of organizational change. Over the past decade I have been increasingly faced with a discrepancy between traditional models of the change process and the actual practice of facilitating change. From my work with other "change agents," including executives, managers, and consultants, it is clear I haven't been alone in experiencing this discrepancy.

In the traditional planned change model of organizational change, success is supposed to hinge on four factors:

1. extensive planning and design
2. precise assessment of the current situation
3. accurate anticipation of resistance to change
4. adeptness at overcoming this resistance

Each of these four factors has important practical implications. It is our conception of the process of organizational change that powerfully shapes how we go on to practice organizational change interventions.

Yet, in my experience not only has it been precisely these four factors which are consistently violated successful change has little to do with either sufficient planning, assessment, anticipation of resistance, or somehow "overcoming" resistance. For instance, no matter how sound the original plans and designs are, I have found they usually need to be scrapped early on in the intervention due to unexpected contingencies like illnesses or transfers of key players, financial crises, and unplanned conflict. These unplanned occurrences also render relatively worthless the second success factor, accurate assessments, since new, unexpected events provoke a set of unprecedented responses not covered in the original assessment.

In terms of the supposed pervasiveness of resistance to change, it has been my growing realization that strong opposition on the part of employees usually signals something wrong with the manner of the intervention, rather than some kind of innate inertia of the employees. However, this also means that overcoming this resistance is simply not to the point. Instead, resistance is something to be worked with as a potentially very fruitful source of insight into the deep-rooted dynamics at work in the situation.

This discrepancy between theory and practice is forcing us to rethink fundamental assumptions about organizational change. We need to ask:

- What exactly is organizational change?

- What is it that is changed?

- How is this change best accomplished?

- What are the appropriate roles and competencies of change agents?

All of these questions ultimately hinge on addressing an even more fundamental question:

- What is the nature of this process of change in a system?

This last has become *the* crucial question. In our modern world of constant, even overwhelming change, where the very survival of our businesses and institutions have become a paramount issue, nothing about change in organizations should any longer be taken for granted!

A REVOLUTIONARY NEW MODEL OF CHANGE

The revolution in my thinking began in 1985 when I came across the concept of *self-organization* presented in the book *Order Out of Chaos* by the Nobel-prize-winning scientist Ilya Prigogine and his colleague Isabelle Stengers.[1] As I then explored further research about self-organization in the broad area of "nonlinear systems theory,"[2] I was startled by what was for me an entirely new way for conceiving the process of change in physical systems. I was particularly struck by four basic features of self-organization that truly stood the traditional concepts of system change on their head:

1. Self-organization is a self-generated and self-guided process. This means change is neither a hierarchically controlled nor an externally driven process.

2. Self-organization moves beyond the idea of a system as an inert mass characterized by an innate resistance to change. Instead, change is the activation of a system's inherent potential for transformation, i.e., its "nonlinearity."

3. Self-organization results from the utilization, even enhancement of random, accidental, and unexpected events. Change, then, is not the suppression of chaos; it is order emerging out of chaos—hence the title of Prigogine's and Stenger's book!

4. Self-organization represents a system undergoing a revolution prompted by far-from-equilibrium conditions. This is vastly different than the traditional model where change is nothing more than a mere shift in system functioning and a subsequent return to equilibrium.

A closer look at each of these four elements will both explain the new terms and show how they portray a completely new way of thinking about change in a system.

FEATURE # 1: SELF-GENERATED CHANGE— NOT HIERARCHICALLY DRIVEN

The first element has to do with the "self" in self-organization. The process of system change following the model of self-organization is clearly not the result of either an external or an internal mandate to change. Instead, transformation is self-generated and self-guiding. Of course, there are certain conditions necessary for self-organization to occur, but these conditions are neither hierarchically driven nor hierarchically controlled.

This self-determining feature of self-organization goes completely against the traditional hierarchical-control model of organizational change, which we can analogously call the "good cop/bad cop" approach. Consider for a moment what typically happens during police interrogations—a pair of police officers may play "good cop/bad cop" to gain a confession. The "bad cop" acts aggressive and pushy to pressure a confession, whereas, the "good cop" acts more accepting and involved to win a confession. Both the "good cop" and the "bad cop," however, share the same assumption: the person they are questioning is guilty and is resisting telling the truth! As a result, they both need to bring about the confession by an external pressure, one more forceful, the other more gentle.

Similarly, there are two basic approaches traditionally used to bring about organizational change: either management pressure or a more gentle approach inspired by the methods of organization development (OD). Implementing organizational change via management pressure is like the "bad cop," the gentler OD approach is like the "good cop." But both approaches share the same presumption that change is a hierarchically driven process. This assumption undergirds how specific change interventions are designed, how change agents are supposed to act and react during the intervention, and how the intended changes are to be sustained after the initial efforts are finished.

Think about how Total Quality Management (TQM) is typically implemented. A company's CEO or other senior executive decides his or her company must have it; the TQM goal is announced at a senior management meeting; the senior managers, in turn, direct their staffs to implement this new objective; the next line of managers then call their own meetings and direct their own staffs; and so on down the organization. Directives are set in motion and pressure to change is brought to bear downward in the organization. In other words, TQM is typically implemented in a top-down and hierarchically imposed fashion.

A successful TQM program, however, requires far-reaching changes in work flow methods, management style, performance evaluation, employee participation, and job design. Isn't there a contradiction between the participatory practices demanded by TQM and the nonparticipatory way many TQM programs are mandated by senior executives? Many organizations, as a matter of fact, have run into just this obstacle: the paradox of trying to command a participatory program by nonparticipatory methods. TQM led to self-organizing change at "Carville General," however, because of the participatory nature of the team charters and the impeachment rules they included.

Of course, most organizations nowadays are smarter than merely resorting to authoritarian directive. Instead, they adopt the planned-change approach of organization development (OD) mentioned above. In this more "enlightened" OD perspective, obvious signs of managerial pressure have indeed disappeared and been replaced by persuasion and participation. Participation in the change process may be encouraged, yet this participation usually consists of organizational structures like project teams that do not usually arise spontaneously from the persons affected by the change, but are instead imposed on them. This is not a self-generating or self-organizing process; hierarchic control is still running the show. Thus, we hear much talk about the necessity of top management intentions and commitment to the change process.

But if the approach to change the organization is characterized by hierarchical control, then it is this hierarchical control which is essentially coming forth, no matter how nonhierarchical the new vision is. Here, good intentions and powerful visions are undermined by means that contradict the message—new wine poured into old wine skins! Sooner or later the contradiction will surface and the new wine will go sour.

Self-organization, however, is not hierarchically driven. Instead it is a process of system transformation that is self-generating. Self-organization happens when a work group or an organization is facing a challenge and is allowed to respond to that challenge in a spontaneous, unshackled manner. The issue, then, is not how to pressure a system to change, but how to unleash the system's self-organizing potential to meet a challenge. But for those accustomed to old ways of thinking about organizational change, this may demand a leap of faith. What is radically new about the self-organization perspective is that a work group or organization as a natural system will spontaneously know how to reorganize in the face of a challenge, *if the obstacles hindering its capacity to self-organize are removed.*

FEATURE # 2: NONLINEARITY, AN INHERENT TENDENCY FOR CHANGE—NOT RESISTANCE

To understand the nature of nonlinearity, let's contrast it with linearity. In recent years, the word "linear" has enjoyed currency as a pejorative label for restrictive or uncreative thinking. "Linear" minds supposedly overrely on left-brain functions like logical thinking. Whereas, "nonlinear" thinking is presumed to be more right-brain and creative. Whatever the merits of this distinction (surely, it's oversimplified!), the terms "linear" and "nonlinear" in this book are not being used in this split-brain fashion. Instead, "linear" and "nonlinear" refer to systems demonstrating either linear or nonlinear mathematical properties, and particularly to how these formal properties relate to the processes of system transformation.[3]

For example, consider these two very different pictures of change. First, a huge locomotive is changing a freight train from one track position to another. The train is an inert, sluggish mass that requires an external force equal to the task to get it moving. This is similar to change conceived in linear terms. Change from a linear perspective is not a potential within the system. Inertia is the basic characteristic of the freight train. Furthermore, because the train is massive, it requires the massive power of a locomotive to move it.

Second, imagine a flower bulb sprouting a leaf in early spring. The bulb contains the future flower as a potential that is activated under the right conditions of soil, air temperature, sunlight, and moisture. This growth potential is analogous to nonlinear change, whereby an inherent potential for change is activated by the right conditions.

Change conceived in a linear way is like the typical picture that comes to mind when envisioning how to increase the productivity standards of a factory work unit. The work unit seems to act as a united entity, a coherent system resisting the change like a freight train. A change is imposed, employees resist, and management tries harder, or tries something different, or tries something different harder!

This *rhythm* of change and resistance looks a lot like someone pushing a donkey to get it to move. Donkeys are notoriously stubborn animals—when pushed, they stiffen instead of moving. In fact, the harder you push, the stiffer the donkey becomes. Of course, no one attributes this stubbornness to the pusher—it's just that donkeys are stupid, stubborn animals!

The donkey model leaves only three options to "overcome" the resistance:

1. *Psyche out the resistors.* Before the change is even initiated, psyche out the potential resistors and disarm them. For example, a crafty manager includes potential resistors in the steering committee to make them feel involved and listened to, and therefore less likely to interfere with the change.

2. *Appeal to higher authority.* Since it was management who originally mandated the change, why not simply overpower the resistance through a show of greater hierarchical power? Or, a common refrain heard from professional change agents is that top management commitment must be visible. But, all too often this top management "commitment" is simply a euphemism for more authoritarian pressure.

3. *Practice the art of friendly persuasion.* Explain the intended change as a benefit to all those involved. For example, employees attend an impressive presentation featuring computer-generated graphics, expert speakers, and promises of all the tremendous benefits that will flow from the intended change. Surely these recalcitrant and unrepentant employees will now see the light!

If the bells and whistles don't work, there is always the tried and true, one-on-one, "I'll take you in my confidence" number. The better the change agent, the more skilled they are in this fine art of friendly persuasion—organizational change becomes a hybrid con-game!

Of course, any of these methods may work, at least in the short run. But how much resentment, ill-will, and distrust are created at the same time? There is always the fourth option: abandon the change effort

altogether! This alternative is more frequently chosen than is readily admitted, when you include allowing new programs to simply die out.

However, an amazing characteristic of nonlinearity in a system is that it contains its own capacity for transformation, requiring only the right conditions for activation. That is, nonlinear systems have locked up within their nonlinearity a tendency toward change, growth, and development. This innate potential is similar to how an entire oak tree is contained in an acorn and only requires the right conditions to emerge. In fact, nonlinear systems are essentially evolving systems, transforming into greater and greater complexity.

In a nonlinear system, resistance to change is merely an aspect of the system's nonlinearity, an aspect that has not yet been channeled in the direction of change or growth. As we shall see later, resistance—at its heart a nonlinear phenomenon—actually contains the seeds of its own transformation!

FEATURE # 3: TRANSFORMATION OUT OF CHAOS—NOT CONTROL STRATEGIES

Research into self-organization has introduced the notion that systems radically transform themselves by taking advantage of random or accidental occurrences. During the process of self-organization, a system varies from its normal mode of functioning in barely noticeable ways that are eventually incorporated into new patterns or new modes of behavior. In other words, a new kind of order emerges out of the unpredicted disorder.

This struck me as a rather remarkable idea—after all, my theoretical stance until then had been that the very nature of ordered patterns, such as the management hierarchy of a corporation, depended on controlling or getting rid of unpredictable variations in functioning. A manager's job is supposed to be about controlling and dampening variances—budget variances, work performance variances, inventory variances. The goal of a good manager has always been to keep the unpredictable and the random to a bare minimum, in other words to maintain the equilibrium.

Planning, prediction, anticipation, and control underlie the whole edifice of *planned change* that has been guiding organizational change interventions for years. However, now we are confronted with a view of system change claiming that deeply rooted change comes about not as the result of abolishing unpredictable variation, but precisely through amplifying it.

I had a sudden insight—these new notions might be speaking to the discrepancy between theory and practice in organizational change that I described earlier. Since organizational change is a type of system change, maybe the key to successful organizational change is related to this idea of taking advantage of the random, the unexpected, and the unpredictable. I already had experienced, as have many others, that organizational change can be unpredictable and often results from taking advantage of random events emerging during the change process.

Departures from equilibrium or the status quo occur all the time in spite of the power of equilibrium-seeking processes. For example, someone at work may come up with a new product idea never tried before, or a person by chance finds a different way to operate a piece of equipment, or someone comes across a new approach to budgeting when reading a magazine in the dentist's office. Most of the time these spontaneous, random events or ideas are quickly dampened and never achieve a significant impact on the organization's operation. The range of available and allowable behavior is simply too limited by the emphasis on control.

Self-organization does just the opposite. Random departures from equilibrium are noticed, encouraged, amplified, and eventually incorporated into the way the work group or organization operates. The new way to do the budget, the new approach to operating the machine, the new product concept are all noticed and encouraged and tried out. This, in fact, is exactly what self-organization is all about: using random or new events to organize the system in a new way.

FEATURE #4: FAR-FROM-EQUILIBRIUM CONDITIONS—NOT MERE SHIFTS IN EQUILIBRIUM

The fourth element of self-organization is the notion that system transformation takes place only in a far-from-equilibrium condition. This was an entirely new concept for me since my theoretical orientation had been an equilibrium-based perspective. Again I wasn't alone in this bias toward equilibrium. The traditional OD approach was based on Kurt Lewin's model of the force-field in which change was seen as a shift from one state of equilibrium to another.[4]

For example, if a factory work group has a productivity output that remains relatively stationary over time, this is considered its equilibrium level. Changing the productivity output is tantamount to shifting the equilibrium to a higher level of productivity. Lewin's model, like that of other social scientists of his day was primarily an equilibrium-based model. Moreover, equilibrium models were at the basis of most ways of approaching systems—from the idea of the balance of nature in ecology and biology, to the crucial role of equilibrium in economics.[5]

Equilibrium traditionally is defined as the state in which a system is at rest or not changing. It is a condition of the lowest organization and complexity. At equilibrium a system seeks to stay the same, continuing its habitual patterns and in a sense constantly repeating the past. The emergence of new patterns of behavior in the system are seen to be in opposition to the deeper, more dominant force of equilibrium.

A major criticism against equilibrium models is that with this tendency toward equilibrium, where nothing is changing, it is not clear how growth and the emergence of novelty can take place.[6] After all, novelty requires the emergence of new patterns that, in their departure from equilibrium, are not eliminated, but are instead allowed to deeply affect the system. This requires the system to move beyond equilibrium into a far-from-equilibrium condition.

Prigogine and others were talking about just this kind of far-from-equilibrium condition. This notion, however, contains none of the negative associations conveyed by *disequilibrium*: a topsy-turvy, vertiginous, stumbling around. Instead, by interrupting equilibrium-seeking processes in a system, a far-from-equilibrium condition need not make the system more disoriented or turbulent. In fact, the opposite may happen, for in a system where the habitual patterns are constantly spinning wheels, persistently shifting priorities, and chronic upheaval, the interruption of equilibrium will be characterized by more stability, coordination, and harmony.

Far-from-equilibrium conditions challenge a nonlinear system to come up with a new way of functioning. A system that predominantly seeks equilibrium is a system that resists change. Such systems allow neither creative development nor innovative response to their environments.

Self-organization demands that a system be in a far-from-equilibrium condition so that the developmental potential of the system is released, just as the right soil conditions release the growth of an acorn. In fact, the need for systems to move beyond equilibrium in order to grow and evolve has prompted contemporary ecologists and biologists to reject the old notion of the "balance of nature" in favor of the idea that nature is a network of systems "out of balance" or far-from-equilibrium. And growth is made possible by far-from-equilibrium conditions interrupting processes that strive to keep a system from changing or developing.[7]

Far-from-equilibrium conditions, then, are just what organizational transformation is all about. They are the conditions that facilitate an organization or work group in coming up with creative, new solutions to the challenges it faces. A model of change based on far-from-equilibrium conditions fits exactly the needs of organizations in a state of rapid flux, where technology changes at lightning speed and companies must innovate or perish.

NEW WINE SKINS WITH NEW ASSUMPTIONS

Self-organization suggests an approach to organizational change that is as revolutionary as the changes now demanded in the work place. This is the new wine skin required for the new wine of reengineering, process innovation, TQM, continuous improvement, new inventory methods, participative work environments, and rewarding and productive organizational cultures. We can no longer conceive of change as a fight against the natural tendency of systems to stay the same. On the contrary, organizations innately tend toward change under the appropriate far-from-equilibrium conditions.

In summary, using self-organization rather than hierarchical imposition as a model for change in work groups and organizations demands that we introduce a new set of assumptions to guide the change process.

- Instead of resisting change, organizations and work groups tend toward change and development.

- Instead of hierarchically imposing change, the potential for change is unleashed and activated.

- Instead of "unfreezing" and "refreezing," a spontaneous reorganization emerges representing a more effective way to accomplish the organization's objectives.

- Instead of large changes requiring large efforts, small-scale efforts can facilitate large scale changes.

- Instead of emphasizing planning, change is an evolving strategy utilizing chance and accidental events.

- Instead of only focusing on what is internal to the organization, the self-organization approach includes the paradoxical work in firming up and traversing the boundaries between a work group or organization and its environment.

- Instead of relying only on a rational and cognitive perspective, change needs to incorporate elements of play and with what may even appear absurd.

- Instead of consensus-seeking as the means toward participation, nonconsensus-seeking can lead to spontaneous participatory structures.

Self-organization takes place when the right kind of system is placed under the right set of circumstances: the right type of system is a *nonlinear* system and the right set of circumstances are *far-from-equilibrium* conditions. The rest of this book explains the ramifications of these two essential components of self-organization, and their impact on the role of change agents.

GROWTH IN NONLINEAR SYSTEMS

Difficult things beneath heaven
Are made up of easy things.
Big things beneath heaven
Are made up of small things.
Thus the sage
Never deals with the great,
But accomplishes greatness.
—TAO TE CHING (63)

Consider the following guidelines that have been accumulating over the years for agents of planned change in organizations.

- Successful change requires extensive planning before actual intervention.

- A critical strategy is to anticipate accurately when and where resistance will emerge.

- When resistance arises don't let it derail your change intentions—the organization ultimately will move in the direction you are pushing it if you have enough endurance, skill, and determination.

- Large-scale changes require large-scale efforts whereas small-scale changes only need small-scale efforts.

At first sight, these seem like reliable guidelines. After all, they are based on the virtues of patience, persistence, foresight, competency, and even common sense.

A second look, however, reveals that they contain certain questionable presuppositions about organizations. The emphasis on planning and anticipation implies that organizations are largely predictable enterprises. The requirement of persistent determination implies that organizations lack an inherent capacity for change. the proportionality between effort and result implies that organizations are inert masses that follow the Newtonian laws of mass, force, and movement.

Predictability, inertia, and proportionality characterize systems that are fundamentally linear. Basing a model of system change on these presuppositions ignores the dynamic, nonlinear aspect of organizations, which may explain why successful change is so rare or short-lived. Self-organization, as a fundamentally new way of conceiving the process of system change, relies on the ideas of a *nonlinear system* and the *far-from-equilibrium conditions* under which a nonlinear system transforms itself. This chapter explores the differences between linear and nonlinear systems, a crucial step toward understanding the process of self-organization.

Nonlinearity itself is not a new concept. Mathematicians and scientists have long realized the importance of nonlinear equations. A new area of research that is so exciting for our purposes in looking at organizational change, however, is concerned with how nonlinear systems hold within themselves a vast potential for transformation. By becoming aware of the behavior, as well as the potential, of nonlinear systems, we will be better able to understand the application of nonlinearity to our new conception of organizational change.

NONLINEAR CHANGE AT "CARVILLE GENERAL HOSPITAL"

Remember, for example, the way that "Carville General Hospital" behaved during the implementation of a TQM program. Initially, three project teams were established, each of which instituted their own ground rules, including meeting format, leadership, and conflict resolution strategies. One of the new ground rules—the rather innocent "starting and ending meetings on time"—had repercussions that went far beyond what anyone had foreseen. In fact, when the CEO on the senior management team violated this little rule, it triggered an entire reorganization of the team's hierarchy, including the impeachment of the CEO from his leadership role on this team. This, in turn, led to a reconsideration of the leadership style of the hospital. The new ground rule challenged the cultural norm of coming to meetings late, a norm derived from a general arrogance on the part of management in which their authority supposedly legitimated all of their actions.

The new rule about coming to meetings on time was introduced at a moment when the organization was primed for change. The necessary conditions for self-organization were present. This small event revealed the powerful effect of nonlinearity in the organization; once unleashed, this event had a disproportionate, unpredictable, and transformative effect on the whole hospital.

FROM LINEAR TO NONLINEAR SYSTEMS

We can better appreciate the unique features of nonlinear systems by contrasting them with linear systems. Since our entire understanding of organizations thus far has been decidedly linear, some of the features of a nonlinear system may at first seem strange or bizarre. But it is exactly these strange features that indicate the enormous power of transformation locked within nonlinear systems. Indeed, one of the great beauties of the new nonlinear sciences is that they better approximate the undeniably irregular, organic, and even counterintuitive behavior of real systems in nature and human culture. We no longer need to understand these systems by putting them into the procrustean bed of linear and equilibrium abstractions.

PRECIPITOUS AND REVOLUTIONARY CHANGE

In linear systems change is gradual and incremental, whereas in nonlinear systems change can be precipitous and revolutionary. Take, for example, money deposited in a savings plan that features only simple interest, a linear process not conducive to getting rich very quickly. Using simple interest the amount accumulated is not added to the original amount, so the interest is only on the original investment.

If you put $1,000 in a savings plan with 10 percent simple interest, for example, at the end of the year, you will have an additional $100 because 10 percent of $1,000 is $100. This $100 is then taken out of the bank, leaving only the original $1,000. Again, at the end of the second year you will have another $100, which you withdraw again. If this is done every year for 10 years you will have made an extra $1,000 at the end of the ten years, which added to the original amount of $1,000 will have doubled your original investment.

Graphing what takes place with simple interest shows that it is a linear process because the growth of the investment over 10 years can be represented as a straight *line*, hence linear (see Figure 2-1).

In contrast to linear simple interest, nonlinear compounded interest offers a better chance of accumulating wealth. Compounding interest consists of adding the money accumulated through interest to the original amount so that interest accumulates on the total amount of the original investment plus the additional amount made by interest. Again, assume you start with a $1,000 investment and the interest rate is 10 percent. Instead of withdrawing the money made by interest at the end

---

Incremental or Revolutionary Business Change?

Researchers into the productivity levels of ten businesses over time found that the productivity levels of some of these businesses showed a precipitous, or nonlinear, change.[1] Some of these changes coincided with large environmental changes, such as the country being at war. Other changes corresponded to changes in internal operation. One company showed a decrease for several years, then a large, precipitous increase that followed a restructuring in which a more efficient work-flow method was introduced.

The pattern of changes suggests that change can occur as incremental growth or as a revolutionary spurt. A nonlinear model can account for both types of development in an organization—the linear and the nonlinear—because the nonlinear contains the linear as a special case.

of each year, you add this amount to the original investment. In the second year the 10 percent interest will accumulate on $1,100, which is the original amount plus the interest from the first year. Every year, then, interest will accrue on a greater amount. At the end of ten years your money will have grown approximately 2.6 times the original amount instead of just doubling. Thus, using compound interest, you will have approximately $2,600 instead of the mere $2,000 you would have gotten from simple interest. That, of course, is why everyone prefers compound over simple interest.

Compound interest is nonlinear since the increase in the total amount of the investment is a rising curve (see Figure 2-2). In other words, change in a nonlinear system occurs more precipitously than in a linear system. The degree of nonlinearity, or how much the nonlinear process differs from the behavior of a linear one, is shown by the steepness of a curve, or how much the curve differs from a straight line.

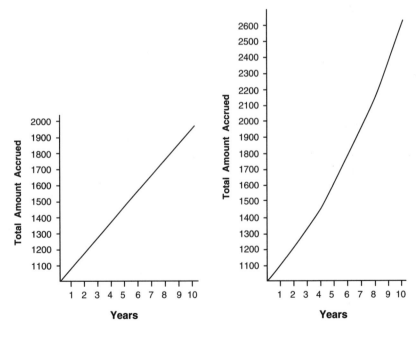

Figure 2-1.
A Linear Graph of
Simple Interest

Figure 2-2.
A Nonlinear Graph of
Compound Interest

DISPROPORTIONALITY

In linear systems the effect is proportionate to the cause, whereas in nonlinear systems the effect is disproportionate to the cause. A look at the graph for simple interest (Figure 2-1) shows that as each year passes, there is a constant, proportionate change in the amount of money. In linear systems, changes in one part of the system are directly proportionate to changes in the other parts of the system.

Proportionality in a linear system implies that a small change in one element in a system has a correspondingly small effect on another element of the system, or that a large change in one element has a correspondingly large effect on another element.

A Huge Linear Intervention at "Colossal Engineering"

Several years ago, "Colossal Engineering," a huge U.S.-based manufacturer of turbines for hydroelectric plants, encountered competition from Japanese and German firms for the first time. Whereas before the corporate culture of this manufacturer was product-driven with a focus on engineering the most efficient turbine, now the firm had to shift its focus to emphasize marketing. This went against the grain of the engineers who dominated the culture.

Looking at the company as a linear system, in which a large-scale project would require a large-scale change effort, top management set up an extensive and elaborate change strategy. Hundreds of consultants were brought in from all over the country to conduct training seminars in marketing orientation as well as to establish marketing project teams with the engineers. The process took one-and-a-half years. At the end of that period, the engineers certainly knew more about marketing, but the problem of competition was barely scratched. Senior managers then decided the required changes exceeded expectations, so they again contracted with even more consultants for further training and other interventions. Of course, by envisioning change linearly, this process of escalating the intervention could go on ad infinitum since the relation of cause and effect must be proportionate. As soon as the changes are seen to be greater than expected, the intervention must also become that much more extensive.

By contrast, in a nonlinear system, the relationship between the elements of the system is disproportionate. Changes in one part or element of the system do not lead to a proportionate change in other parts of the system. A small change may have a large effect, and a large change may have a small effect.

What happened at "Carville General Hospital" was nonlinear: a small intervention, the rule of starting the meeting on time, had a disproportionately large effect that changed the way power was distributed in the hierarchy and led to an authentic participative structure in the top management team. Of course, the small intervention did not take place in a void. Conditions had been set in motion that enabled the small change to become an influential factor. This is how far-from-equilibrium conditions prompt self-organization: they allow the inherent nonlinearity in the system to manifest itself.

THE WHOLE IS GREATER THAN THE SUM OF THE PARTS

In linear systems the whole is merely the sum of the parts, whereas in nonlinear systems, the whole is greater than the sum of the parts. This distinction goes right to the heart of what a *system* is all about: A system is not merely a conglomeration of parts like a heap of stones on a beach. The word *system* implies that its parts are interrelated and interactive, perhaps even in such a way that the system contains potentials not inherent in the parts by themselves.

Going back to the example of simple interest again, if two separate bank accounts with $1,000 and $500 respectively are combined, obviously more money will accumulate interest. The final amount in the combined account, however, will not exceed the sum of final total amount in the two accounts had they been kept separate. In other words, the sum of two solutions is again a linear solution.

This example shows simply that in linear systems the whole is just the sum of the parts, neither more nor less. It also shows that changes applied to parts or elements in a linear system do not build up disproportionately. If you change the parts, the whole changes only in the same proportion as the parts are to the whole. Accordingly, in a linear system, a small change in one of the elements of the system has only a small effect on the system as a whole.

Changing the Parts but Not the System at "PsychCare"

At "PsychCare," a psychiatric care facility in the Southwest, the nursing department operated according to a set of procedural manuals that hadn't been revised for 20 years. Furthermore, the nursing units operated as closed systems by not communicating with the rest of the hospital. The result was that general hospital information didn't seem to reach the staff nurse.

The entire medical center was undergoing a major transition to institute a Total Quality Management program. The nursing department, however, would have no part of it. After all, TQM principles didn't fit in with the 20-year-old procedures manual. The Director of Nursing was so upset by the transition that she took early retirement, which left the top management of the medical center hoping that now change could finally take place.

Management's tacit assumption, however, was that changes occur linearly, like changing the tracks of a freight train. In this case the linear change strategy was based on the assumption that if you replace a manager, the system under the control of the manager should also change.

A young new director was appointed from outside who had shown during her interview and through past experience that she was creative and visionary in her approach to managing the nursing department. After only a short time, however, the old patterns resurfaced and the same "us-versus-them" mentality reasserted itself. The new director began to be as controlling and information-filtering as the previous director. It seemed that the whole was really more than the sum of the parts at "PsychCare," and even though parts of the system had changed, the system as a whole was continuing its old patterns.

What happened was that the system's nonlinearity had reared its head. It would take more to transform this system than a locomotive pushing and pulling a freight train.

A nonlinear system is not a mere conglomeration of parts, but also includes the system of relationship between the parts, making it a whole system. The parts interact in such a way that as the system coalesces it has a reality above and beyond the collection of its parts. In later chapters, more will be said about this dynamic aspect of whole systems.

Understanding the behavior of whole systems requires going beyond a simple understanding of adding parts together. Analyzing a system into constituent parts and simply grouping them together does not suffice for understanding the dynamics of a whole system.

MULTIDIRECTIONAL INTERACTION

In linear systems interaction is only one-way, whereas in nonlinear systems interaction is multidirectional. In the example of simple interest, interest accumulates as the result of a simple mathematical operation. At the end of the year, the interest is taken out of the bank and the original amount of the principal remains. This means the causal arrow in the process of accumulating interest is only one-way. The interest is directed to the principal every year, but the principal is never directed back onto the interest.

In a linear system, the elements are seen to have only this one-way influence. Although one element may influence a new state in another element, this other element does not, as a result of this new state, simultaneously influence the first element back again. That is, no mutually reinforcing effect takes place.

Interdivisional Competition at "U.S.A. Motors"

Nonlinear mutual interaction can be seen in how conflict escalated between two divisions at a major automobile manufacturer. Division "Elite" produced "U.S.A. Motors" luxury car, whereas Division "Efficiency" manufactured a subcompact. Tension between the divisions was nothing new: historically they competed for higher funding, R&D budgets, and receiving the limelight from corporate headquarters.

The conflict became severe in 1990 during the Gulf War when car sales plummeted. Each division geared up internal campaigns claiming that, after the war, consumers would buy their respective cars. But as each division pumped up their lobbying efforts at the corporate level, they came to see each other as belligerent. As the competition and accusations intensified, more effort went into proving that the other division was *way off* in their market research. This, however, prompted even greater counterefforts, with the result that the company's priorities suffered. Thus a nonlinear mutual interaction occurred whereby expectations, behavior, and outcome escalated into destructive conflict.

Schnauzers and Mice: A Nonlinear System

For an example of a nonlinear, multidirectional relationship among the elements of a system, imagine a system of animals living in the same region. Some animals are predators, others are prey. Just for the sake of a vivid picture, assume the prey are mice and the predators are miniature schnauzer dogs. The scene is set on a large farm where many mice are eating up the crops. A few schnauzers, males and females, are set loose to stop the crop damage. Assume that mice and schnauzers are the only two species, the mice eating crops and the schnauzers only eating mice.

When the schnauzers are first set loose, there are plenty of mice. Since the schnauzers have lots of food, they fare well, and over the course of time they multiply. As the population of schnauzers goes up, the population of mice goes down. As more and more mice are eaten, however, there is less food for the schnauzers, and they eventually die from starvation. But with fewer schnauzers, the mice have fewer enemies, so the mice start to thrive and multiply. But when this happens, there is more food for the schnauzers, so they stop starving and start thriving again. There is a nonlinear, circular relationship between the population of schnauzers as predators and mice as prey.

In the case of compound interest, the interest is continually added to the original amount so that interest accrues on the original investment plus the extra amount, thereby making the direction of causality mutual between the operation of interest and the amount operated on.

Mutual causality is a feedback process that continually pumps the effect of an operation back into the operation.[2] Each subsequent performance of the operation occurs under conditions different from the previous one. An example of feedback is the irritating screech that sometimes bursts out of public address system speakers during a concert or speech. The screech occurs when a microphone that is placed too close to a speaker picks up any sound that comes out of the speaker, then sends the sound back to the speaker. The speaker amplifies this sound, which the microphone then picks up again and sends to the speaker in amplified form. Around and around the sound goes, each time being amplified until it escalates into a blood-curdling shriek. If the process was simply linear and didn't involve amplification, then the sound would just get gradually louder.

UNPREDICTABLE OUTCOMES

Linear systems have predictable outcomes, whereas nonlinear systems may have unpredictable outcomes. Predicting how much money you would have accumulated a century from now would be easy to do if you were using simple interest. Assuming you had a large enough piece of paper, all you would need to do is follow the line that depicts the linear relationship between the original and the eventual investment.

Because of proportionality and the whole being perceived as merely the sum of the parts, the eventual outcome of linear systems is very predictable. The straight line doesn't change, so you can extend it indefinitely by finding the values of one variable from the value of the other as far along the graph as you desire. There is no mystery; everything is evident from the line on the graph that depicts the relationship between the two variables.

Since prediction is one of the hallmarks of scientific enterprise, scientists have been intent on reducing the mathematics of system behavior to linear equations. The classical worldview of science presumed that the future states of any linear system could be predicted by applying relevant linear operations to measurements of the system at some initial time.[3] In this spirit of classical predictability, Kurt Lewin, the progenitor of organization development, could assert that social behavior was predictable if all the forces affecting an individual were known.[4] Difficulties in prediction in nonlinear equations have been a reason why scientists shunned them in the past.

Why Is the Weather So Hard to Predict?

The spring of 1992 in New York was particularly dismal. Cold winter temperatures, even a few snow storms, persisted into spring. "The sun will be out over the weekend!" the TV weatherman exclaimed on Friday. But, Saturday morning came along and it was still gloomy—the same for the afternoon, and Sunday was no better. It seemed the weatherman just didn't have a clue.

In this day of supercomputers and advanced satellite technology, why should it be so hard to predict the weather? Of course, there are numerous and complicated factors to take into consideration: the jet stream; ocean currents and temperatures; sunspot activity; environmental pollution; wind speeds; and so on.

At first glance, it seems that all those complicating factors make the weather so unpredictable. Therefore, paring the weather down to just a few simple elements in an ideal model ought to improve the predictability, at least, of the abstract system. In 1963, meteorologist Edward Lorenz did just that—he created an abstract model of the weather by reducing it to three simple equations having to do with air currents and temperature.[5]

Working with just three equations, Lorenz made a fantastic discovery: it was *mathematically impossible* to predict the weather more than a few days in advance. That it was going to be hot in August (in northern latitudes) was still predictable, but it was unpredictable whether it would rain or be sunny on a particular day. This blew apart the old dream that eventually, with enough data and enough data-processing capacity in computers, the weather could be predicted with perfect accuracy.

Lorenz came to realize the unpredictability was the result of the *nonlinear* way that the various factors and forces interact to produce

particular weather phenomena, especially in terms of mutual causality. For example, the speed of air currents influences air temperature while, at the same time, the air temperature influences the speed of air currents. As a result, an increase of the speed of the current leads to an increase in temperature. The increased temperature leads to the heat being transmitted faster, which causes the temperature to increase faster, and so on around in a mutually causal circle. This mutual causality is nonlinear. This kind of mutually reinforcing and escalating causality is dramatically exhibited in the intense self-organizing effects of a quick-building thunderstorm on a hot and humid day.

With all of these nonlinear interactions, it is no wonder that the weather is said to include the extremely nonlinear "butterfly effect" made famous by chaos theory. The butterfly effect refers to how air currents from a butterfly flapping its wings in Asia are amplified to influence the weather in North America! The extreme disproportion between the tiny butterfly wing currents and the entire weather of North America attests to the extremely nonlinear character of the weather.

LINEAR SYSTEMS AT EQUILIBRIUM

Linear systems at equilibrium conditions remain the same, whereas nonlinear systems at far-from-equilibrium conditions can undergo transformation. When a system is under equilibrium conditions, nothing much is taking place; everything is pretty much at rest. That is why linear equations are useful for understanding the dynamics of systems at equilibrium—changes are only gradual and they are proportional to their causes. In fact, as mathematician Ian Stewart put it, the docility of linear equations led classical mathematicians to concentrate mainly on systems in or near equilibrium where linearity is sufficient, such as shallow waves, low-amplitude vibrations, or small temperature differences.[6] This temptation to treat all systems as linear systems at or near equilibrium conditions was so strong that departures from equilibrium were consistently downplayed in importance, and were treated with linear methods.[7] That is, the relationships between the elements of the system are confined to behavior that is congruent with linearity.

Nonlinear systems are not static; they change and evolve when the appropriate far-from-equilibrium conditions are met. Indeed, such a perspective regards the static condition of equilibrium merely as an initial phase of many more interesting phases that the system moves through when it is taken into a far-from-equilibrium process.

This far-from-equilibrium process is important for our purpose because of the inherent *growth potential* that shows itself as a nonlinear system evolves under appropriate nonequilibrium conditions. This kind of nonlinearity is more than the exponential increase associated with compound interest; it reflects a potential for development that allows for the emergence of new structures, patterns, and means for achieving the system's objectives.

The evolution of a nonlinear system is marked by a series of phases, each of which is ruled by a reigning *attractor.* These attractors are analogous to stages of human development: infancy, childhood, adolescence, adulthood. Each stage has its own unique characteristic set of behaviors, tasks to be accomplished, patterns of thinking, activation of emotions, and so on. Though a child sometimes acts like an adult, the long-term behavior of the child is childlike. Similarly, the long-term behavior of a system operating within a specific attractor regime is the kind of behavior associated with that attractor.

Chapter 4 goes into much greater detail about attractors and how they relate to so-called resistance to change. For now what needs emphasis is that nonlinear systems under far-from-equilibrium conditions have the potential to evolve into other possible configurations.

The existence of different attractor regimes is not something added to the original nonlinear equation. The really interesting thing about attractors is that they exist in latent form in the original nonlinear equation. As the equations pass through far-from-equilibrium conditions, the various attractor potentials are released. In this way, we can say that the far-from-equilibrium conditions release the inherent attractor potentials locked in the nonlinear relationships in the system.

When the relationships among the elements in a system are nonlinear rather than linear, it follows that the dynamic possibilities for the system are radically different from the behavior of a linear system. In fact, nonlinearity in a system is a precondition for the kind of system behavior that was previously discussed as self-organization. Self-organization cannot take place in a linear system.

The new possibilities of behavior entailed by nonlinearity demand a rethinking of the process of change in nonlinear systems. Change is a completely different matter for a nonlinear system than for a linear system. Since human systems, including organizations and work groups, are decidedly nonlinear in the way their elements are related to one another, the processes of change in human systems cannot be adequately understood using the linear concept that guides traditional approaches to organizational change.

Summary of the Properties of Nonlinearity

- Precipitous change
- Disproportionality
- The whole is greater than the sum of the parts
- Multidirectionality and mutual interaction
- Unpredictable outcomes
- Growth potential

ADVANTAGES OF A NONLINEAR MODEL OVER A LINEAR MODEL

Viewing change as the evolution of nonlinear systems offers several advantages over a linear model. First of all, a nonlinear view takes into account the powerful, mutual causal interactions within an organization. While a linear model assumes the parts of an organization are assembled as a mere collection, a nonlinear model assumes a vital interdependence actually occurring among the elements of an organization. A linear viewpoint does not account for these types of interactions. As a result, it erects change strategies that often fail because they do not address the counterintuitive responses of organizations to change—responses that result from the nonlinear interdependence among the parts of the organization.[8]

Another way to talk about nonlinear interdependence is to focus on the *systemic* nature of work groups or organizations. A nonlinear perspective gives full credence to the crucial role played by the system as the network of relationships among the members of a work group or organization. Thus, in a work team in which all members synergistically work as a cohesive team in solving problems, generating new ideas, and so on, there is a systemic dimension that cannot be explained by breaking the system down into the behavior of the individuals. A linear model cannot account for this type of systemic synergy.

In a nonlinear system, the behavior that emerges is qualitatively different from the behavior in a linear system. There is a greater coherence, correlation, coordination, and flow of information across the parts of the system. Collective behavior is entirely different from the accumulation of individual behavior. In fact, it is only through nonlinear understanding that a work group or organization actually behaves as a system. Nonlinear transformation repatterns these relationships and reorganizes the system.

Finally, a nonlinear system has the potential for self-organization, whereas a linear system does not. The potential for transformation is already innate in the system, in its nonlinear composition. Change does not need to be imposed; it simply needs to be released under the appropriate far-from-equilibrium conditions. Therefore, the kinds of radical organizational change that such strategies as reengineering, cycle time management, concurrent engineering, TQM, and continuous improvement call for are more in line with the deeply rooted nature of spontaneous systemic reorganization found in the self-organization picture of change than in the kind of limited change possible with an approach that is linear-based.

Trying to transform a nonlinear system using a linear model just doesn't work. If organizations are nonlinear, then only a nonlinear strategy takes advantage of organizational nonlinearity with its evolutionary potential.

THE DYNAMICS OF
SELF-ORGANIZATION

Changelessness is a sign of death,
transformation a sign of life.
—COMMENTARY ON THE I CHING BY LAMA ANAGARIKA GOVINDA

Consider for a moment these features of self-organization: radical reorganization of the structure of a system; the spontaneous emergence of novel patterns and configurations; the amplification and incorporation of random events; the discovery of creative alternatives for functioning; and the arising of new coherence and coordination among the parts of the system. These features, which characterize a truly radical transformation of systems, make self-organization a tantalizing new area of scientific research.

Far from being just an interesting scientific curiosity, these features also invite a reconsideration of the entire process of organizational change. To survive, our businesses and institutions must change radically. Recognition and use of the principles of self-organization and nonlinearity offer organizations the tools they need to guide them through successful transformation. Let's look at an example of this kind of radical organizational change.

SELF-ORGANIZATION AT "NATIONAL ELECTRO-COMM"

Three years ago, the effectiveness of the Research and Development Division of "National Electro-Comm," a *Fortune* 100 communications giant, seriously deteriorated: departments operated as isolated fiefdoms, morale was poor, and managers spent most of their time placing blame. R&D's top management considered several options for turning around this situation. First, to overcome the departmental isolation, they could conduct OD-inspired interdepartmental team-building. Second, to remedy the managerial scapegoating, they could institute an extensive divisionwide management development program. Third, to analyze why morale was so low, they could conduct an employee attitude survey and run survey feedback sessions. Fourth, they could install a new incentive system. All of these constitute a linear model, but they instead took a nonlinear approach.

Before setting any of these interventions in motion, they hired two consultants to assess the current situation and plan for changes. The consultants discovered that although department heads showed up at mandatory divisional meetings, there was very little real communication among them. The higher-echelon staff blamed the lower-paid administrators and secretaries for having too much power and using this power in arbitrary and self-serving ways. The vice president in charge of R&D, though promoted into the position for his expertise as a technical innovator, was not all that comfortable with his leadership role. He saw his leadership task as being a caretaker of his staff and therefore he spent a lot of his time smoothing ruffled feathers and seeking harmony.

The project got off to a traditional start. The consultants

- conducted assessment interviews and a survey

- designed a retreat emphasizing consensus-seeking tasks

- used force-field analysis to ascertain resistance to change

- developed a meeting format for group decision-making and problem-solving

- planned for conflict resolution training and practice

- arranged intergroup meetings between departments

During their initial assessment, however, the consultants realized that there was an important connection between the leader's management style and the problems that characterized R&D. The VP's caretaker role set up a self-fulfilling prophecy. The only way his subordinates could get his attention was by creating crises that he, as their caretaker, could resolve. This was most glaringly evident in how the vice president constantly acted as a caretaker for the head of operations for the division, a woman who seemed to manifest a great deal of troubled behavior. Moreover, the fact that the head of operations was a woman only added fuel to the fire of the self-fulfilling prophecy since the prevailing organizational culture among the engineers and scientists in the division assumed that women were indeed creatures in need of caretaking.

In contrast, the organizational culture was characterized by a strong individualistic spirit of expertise among the engineers and scientists that went directly against the caretaking role of the vice president. This individualism seemed to be exaggerated in the sense of isolation between the members of the division, between the departments in the division, and between the R&D division and the rest of "National Electro-Comm."

At the retreat, the vice president ran the meeting. The first day the group had the task of designing its own organizational effectiveness survey. On the second day, the group planned for the next half of the year. Once the process began, the two change agents stopped speaking to the group at all. Instead, they spoke only to the vice president in whispers that were loud enough for everyone else in the room to hear. Using these loud whispers, the consultants interpreted to the vice president what was going on in the group. Thus, one of the consultants would run over to the vice president and tell him in loud stage whispers, "When you are acting patient and listening tolerantly to the person who just interrupted you, you are sending a signal to the system as a whole that everyone can interrupt anyone else."

The absurdity of the intervention consisted in the fact that the consultants comments were obviously not privately communicated to the vice president himself. The intervention intentionally mixed up the levels of communication by melding and confusing the realms of private and public, listening and eavesdropping, and one listener versus the whole group.

The dramatic and theatrical nature of the intervention reached a high point at the end of the second day of the retreat, when the consultants presented the vice president, in front of the whole group, with a scepter and crown, and told the entire group the story of the movie *The Lion in Winter*. At one point in this movie, the king, played by Peter O'Toole, exclaimed, "I do so love to be the King!" On accepting the scepter and crown, the vice president was to repeat the King's refrain of

"I do so love to be the King" three times. The vice president was also told to begin each meeting over the next three months with this refrain.

The lasting result was a major change in the R&D Division. Scape-

goating and blaming ceased. In a self-organizing fashion departments spontaneously began to establish communication channels with each other and with departments outside the division, although this was not part of the formal agenda during the two-day retreat or the follow-up meetings. In fact, managers and departments outside of R&D began to interact with R&D more often as if R&D had become a magnet that attracted and exchanged ideas with the rest of the organization. This spontaneous regrouping of energy, the reorganization of the way business was done, the release of creativity, the activation of the system's inherent resources, and the proliferation of the effects throughout the system are a striking example of the process of self-organization. Self-organization offers managers and other change agents a powerful model to guide organizational transformation.

THE PROCESS OF SELF-ORGANIZATION

Self-organization emerges in nonlinear systems that develop the right far-from-equilibrium conditions. The way that self-organization radically transforms a system, however, runs counter to the popular idea that systems either resist change or end up in total disorder.

Most of us find it difficult to let go of this popular conception of system behavior. Think, for example, of boiling water. As the water heats up, nothing remarkable seems to occur. Eventually, however, when the water gets hot enough, bubbles pop up here and there, and as the water gets still hotter, boiling erupts in an apparently turbulent manner. It seems the water has simply gone from an initial state of resistance to a disorganized tumult.

Laboratory studies reveal, however, that when certain liquids are heated in certain ways highly organized patterns emerge in the liquids that reveal their capacity for self-organization. An elementary but highly instructive example is the Benard liquid that Nobel Prize winner Ilya Prigogine and his associate Gregoire Nicolis studied extensively.[1] By looking at the transformation in the Benard system as a prototype for self-organization, we can appreciate how self-organization presents a fundamentally new understanding of how systems change, and therefore, how it provides a better model to guide the process of organizational change.

SPONTANEOUS AND RADICAL REORGANIZATION

The Benard system is really quite simple: a liquid in a flat, disc-like, glass container, closed on the top, is heated from the bottom. After reaching a critical temperature, the Benard liquid spontaneously restructures itself into highly organized patterns called Benard cells that continue to form as long as the heating continues, as shown in Figure 3-1.

The emergence of the self-organizing Benard cells is analogous to what often happens on a humid summer afternoon: a foggy haze differentiates into definite cloud formations that exhibit pattern and structure. The pattern and structure of the Benard cells shows a new coherence among parts of the system to another. The different parts of the liquid are now, so to speak, communicating this pattern with one another in order to form and maintain the new, intricate structure.

The self-organizing patterns that emerge in the Benard liquid indicate a radical change in the functioning of the system. This change is accomplished not by a hierarchically imposed mandate on the system, nor by any other method of overcoming the system's resistance, but by self-organizing change. This change is self-directed, self-generated, and self-guided as the system reconfigures its own resources in the face of a far-from-equilibrium challenge, which in this particular case, is heat.

But, wait! Isn't the change brought about in the Benard system the result of an external force being imposed on the system, that is, the heat

Figure 3-1. The Highly Structured Patterns of Benard Cells Are an Example of Self-Organization

Source: Adapted from Gregoire Nicolis, "Physics of Far-from-Equilibrium Systems and Self-Organization." In Paul Davies, ed., *The New Physics* (Cambridge: Cambridge Univ. Press), p. 318

being applied to the system? How can you say that this is *self*-organization and not some imposed kind of change? This is an important question, and addressing it can help us understand what exactly is taking place during self-organization.

Heat is applied to the Benard liquid, and to be sure this heat is external to the system. What the system is doing in response to the heat, however, is of the system's *own doing*, a result of the liquid's potential to respond to the heat entering the liquid. Remember that self-organization requires that certain conditions be in place for the nonlinear transformative potential of a system to be activated. In the case of the Benard liquid, the necessary far-from-equilibrium condition is the application of heat to one side of the system. Self-organization is the system's response to a challenge or a new condition.

It might be argued analogously that managerial pressure on a work unit is the necessary condition to get a work unit to change. Certainly, that could be the case if a linear type of change is wanted. But changing direction and radical transformation are two very different things. Linear change is sometimes called for, but if deep-rooted reorganization and re-engineering are required, then self-organization is necessary. At "National Electro-Comm," the consultants' stage whispers and the kingly ritual served as the conditions that challenged the equilibrium-seeking behavior of the group. These two interventions were clearly not any kind of management pressure to change. The far-from-equilibrium conditions that resulted allowed "National Electro-Comm" to spontaneously reorganize. Let's take a look at another example of how an organizational change reveals similar elements of self-organization.

Self-Organization at a City Agency

A spontaneous reorganization also took place during an organizational change process at the "Area Research in Business Collective (ARBCO)," a clearinghouse that provides information for an urban community about small business loans, free or inexpensive business consulting, and fund-raising sources. Because of "ARBCO's" success, the staff became overwhelmed with demands. As a result, the director worked with two external consultants to institute an organizational change process, including a two-day retreat. An unexpected consequence of the retreat was the spontaneous division of the steering committee into subgroups, each of which would be responsible for different "ARBCO" activities. This spontaneous, self-organizing restructuring greatly expedited a more livable work environment.

It is important to note here that this structure was not imposed on "ARBCO" as the result of a top-management plan. In the wake of the quality movement, participative structures or work teams are increasingly imposed on many organizations. Such teams seem to be a good idea, especially in relation to the clumsy, slow-moving hierarchies of most companies. A critical issue, however, is whether these structures and teams are being hierarchically imposed, or whether they are emerging spontaneously as the result of a self-organizing process. The former is just more of the "new wine in old wine skins" mentioned in Chapter 1 and includes all of the limitations that accompany such hierarchically controlled change. The latter, however, does not need reinforcement or refreezing since it will be a spontaneous and natural outgrowth of the work group's activities.

ACTIVATING NONLINEARITY

The self-organizing Benard cells are a curious matter. Before heating, the Benard liquid is in an equilibrium condition. This means it looks pretty much the same from one part to another. The liquid rests in its container, isolated and protected from any kind of environmental influence. This condition of equilibrium is similar to the factory work unit described in Chapter 1. It is a system that resists any attempt to increase productivity output; the standard stays approximately the same no matter what variations occur in absenteeism, scheduling, equipment breakdown, pay increases, shipping rates, or supervisory exhortations. When heat is first applied to the Benard liquid, it is transferred in a linear fashion throughout the system. To maintain equilibrium in the Benard liquid, heat is transferred in a linear fashion throughout the liquid. This is similar to what takes place in a heating pad. After turning on a heating pad, you have to wait while the heat spreads gradually and evenly through the pad. As a result the way heat is spread maintains the equilibrium.

Similarly, because the spread of heat in the Benard liquid at low temperatures is a gradual and even process, it doesn't upset the equilibrium of the liquid. At a critical temperature, however, the Benard liquid is challenged to come up with a better way of transferring heat. There is too much heat at the bottom of the liquid, causing a huge difference in temperature within the liquid. Following nature's propensity to find the most efficient path, the liquid finds a nonlinear method of heat transfer: convection—the emergence of the Benard cells.

It is crucial to recognize that this new nonlinear method of heat transfer was always a potential of the Benard liquid. That is because the essential nature of the Benard liquid is characterized by nonlinear relationships among the elements of the system. At equilibrium conditions this essential nonlinearity does not reveal itself, since linear processes are

sufficient at low temperatures. But under the far-from-equilibrium conditions of the critical temperature, this inherent nonlinearity emerges as the system reorganizes itself into convection cells. Actually, in the Benard and other nonlinear systems, linearity is simply what nonlinearity looks like when equilibrium conditions dominate. In a manner of speaking, nonlinearity is hiding behind linearity until it is confronted by a big enough challenge to come out from hiding and show what it can do.

In the self-organization model of system change, equilibrium and linear processes represent only the initial phase in a developmental sequence of the system's evolution. When the system is under far-from-equilibrium conditions, equilibrium and linearity cease to dominate the system. The real nature of a nonlinear system is its capacity for growth, development, and change. An example of this nonlinear growth can be seen at a state-of-the-art manufacturing firm in Brazil.

Nonlinear Self-Organization at Semco

The manner in which far-from-equilibrium conditions activate the inherent nonlinearity of a system during organizational change becomes particularly clear when there is an escalation and proliferation of change after an initial period of slow growth. For example, at Semco, a fast-growing manufacturing firm in Brazil, the initial change strategies of diversification and professionalization of the work environment led only to a gradual, linear type of change, even though a great deal of effort had gone into the changes.[2] From the point of view of nonlinear systems, these two strategies were *not* acting as far-from-equilibrium conditions with the capacity to unshackle and unleash the nonlinear, self-organizing potential of the system.

Radical transformation did occur at Semco, however, in response to a new set of conditions that challenged the system in fundamental ways. For example, a policy of sharing financial information with all employees was instituted. Semco, however, did not assume that employees would be able to understand and assimilate this financial information. Training programs were established for reading and interpreting the information, and now every employee receives monthly balance sheets, profit and loss analyses, and cash-flow figures.

Certainly this policy was the result of a top management mandate, and could be seen as another example of hierarchical control. *It is important to note, however, that the self-organization model does not elim-*

inate hierarchy or the need for leaders to be leaders. The paradox here is that hierarchical control was used to relinquish control, in the sense that control is often characterized as the hoarding of financial (and other kinds of) information. An open policy on information directly challenges the traditional management practice of operating as a secret society that keeps employees in the dark. This open policy generated a far-from-equilibrium condition by increasing the flow of information in a system, which research has shown is a characteristic of systems undergoing self-organization.[3]

This new policy of shared information was accompanied by other new conditions: employees and managers were able to choose their own job titles and decision-making responsibility was authentically pushed downward. These conditions helped to facilitate nonlinear escalation of change. For example, when the marine division needed a bigger plant, several employees found three potential sites. The plant was closed, and all the employees piled into buses to look at the sites. Afterward, everyone voted on the site to which they wanted to move the plant. This increase in employee involvement in major decision making was certainly not the result of a linear process!

INTERRUPTING EQUILIBRIUM-SEEKING TENDENCIES

When the temperature of the Benard liquid reaches a critical level, something interferes with the tendency of the system to stay the same. The external heat source generates large temperature differences between the liquid that is near the heat source at the bottom of the container, and the liquid at the top of the container that is away from the heat source. The amount of heat in the liquid near the heat source seeks to move to the rest of the liquid faster than a linear heat spread allows. The ability of the system to deal with the heat source by a linear spread of heat becomes strained.

To visualize this, imagine it's a hot day, and a lot of people have come to a public beach accessible only by a narrow walkway. As the walkway becomes more crowded, and people become hotter, many will experience strain and frustration. Perhaps some of the beachgoers will seek another access, such as jumping over the fence and running across the dunes.

The buildup of a heat gap in the Benard liquid is a far-from-equilibrium condition that confronts the system with the necessity of reorganizing itself to spread heat in a more effective manner, like the beachgoers finding a new way to the beach. It is this far-from-equilibrium condition that releases the potential for self-organization in the liquid.

Interfering with Equilibrium at "Guided Systems"

"Guided Systems" is a defense contractor that manufactures computer components for fighter jets and guided missiles. In recent years the competition became severe enough to prompt a reevaluation of the engineering and science-oriented organizational culture. The company needed to become more market- and customer-driven. This scenario is similar to the situation at "Colossal Engineering" mentioned in Chapter 2, where corporate culture change was approached in a linear manner that demanded a huge effort.

At "Guided Systems," however, a more nonlinear and self-organizing approach was introduced. One of the interventions was a program in which the engineers and scientists were asked to challenge the assumptions that underlie traditional ways of making decisions and solving problems. Included were creativity exercises in which totally unrelated ideas and images were juxtaposed with immediate decisional concerns. For example, the word *cat* might be contrasted with the need to get products designed by a deadline. These creativity exercises were not devoted to new product development. They were instead indirectly aimed at the culture of the company.

These exercises interrupted the engineers' customary approach to solving production problems, which typically included problem identification, mathematical analysis, and finally design. Such scientific processes were an aspect of the organization's equilibrium. The exercises opened a large gap between fantasy and reality, between imagination and practical matters, that challenged the equilibrium of this scientifically oriented company. In other words, the exercises generated a far-from-equilibrium situation at "Guided Systems" when the cognitive processes and attitudes underlying science and engineering were interrupted. More examples of equilibrium-busting at "Guided Systems" is explored in Chapter 9.

UTILIZING DEPARTURES FROM EQUILIBRIUM

One of the results of the heat applied to the Benard system is the creation of density differences in the liquid. The following example explains what density is. A warm bottle of beer fizzles over when you open it because heat lowers the density of the beer. Density refers to how closely packed a substance's molecules are to each other (see Figure 3-2). For example, helium gas compressed in a tank has its molecules more densely packed than the outside atmosphere. When the gas is released into a balloon, however, the molecules spread out and the density decreases. When beer becomes warm, the molecules are not as closely packed and, accordingly, the space between the molecules expands. When the bottle is opened, then the beer gushes out.

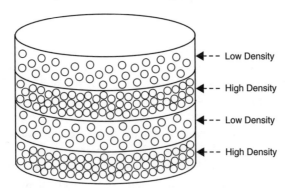

Figure 3-2. Density Differences

When Benard liquid is heated, the temperature of the liquid varies, depending on its proximity to the heat source. The density of the liquid also corresponds to temperature differences: lower density nearer the heat source and higher densities away from the heat. This difference in density and temperature sets up a far-from-equilibrium condition that amplifies small random currents in the liquid.

Gazing at the mirrorlike surface of a calm pond may give the impression that the water in the pond is in a state of total quiescence. If you could peer under the surface, however, you would detect small currents moving around haphazardly. The existence of such currents is characteristic of liquids: unlike solids, no matter how calm the liquid appears, there are slight, moving, hardly noticeable currents.

Similarly, inside the Benard liquid are small, subtle currents that move randomly around the liquid. At low temperatures, when equilibrium dominates the system, the currents are just microscopic departures from the sameness of equilibrium and constantly displace small regions of liquid throughout the container. In this state equilibrium is maintained.

As the currents move around, they may randomly push a small region of the lower-density liquid near the heat source upward toward the cooler liquid. Similarly, a random current of cooler liquid may move downward. These displacements are only small departures from the liquid's equilibrium sameness. At their minuscule level they are hardly noticeable and have no real impact. Thus, in the equilibrium conditions of low heat, the liquid ignores these minute departures from equilibrium.

When the liquid is in a far-from-equilibrium state, however, the effects of random currents are magnified and minuscule currents become nonlinearly amplified. Through the capacity for self-organization, these currents are used, rather than ignored. A small volume of lower-density liquid, displaced by a random current, may find itself in a denser region as it moves upward away from the heat source. Under far-from-equilibrium conditions, the speed at which the currents displace the small volume of liquid upward will be intensified. At the same time, an opposite effect may happen in the upper, colder, denser part of the liquid: small downward currents propel the higher-density liquid downward.

Self-organized system change encourages the recognition and amplification of what is different from equilibrium. The system needs to be primed, so to speak, to take advantage of anything that exhibits a departure from equilibrium. These departures represent creative alternatives to the system's behavior at equilibrium. Therefore, these departures are amplified toward a creative advance on the part of the system.

Going beyond Equilibrium at NEC

Ikujiro Nonaka's recounting of how the Japanese electronics firm NEC got into the business of producing personal computers illustrates the important role of using departures from equilibrium to help transform organizations.[4] Before NEC started manufacturing PCs, the company primarily manufactured products with long life cycles made to the specifications of Nippon Telegraph and Telephone Public Corporation.

To promote sales of semiconductor devices, a new product development group decided to make and sell Japan's first kit for microcomputers, which they then displayed at one of the company's service centers. This was a significant departure from the company's previous equilibrium in two ways: they began to manufacture items that were no longer based on specifications from NTTPC and they began to sell to the public at large.

Surprisingly, a wide range of potential customers were interested in the kits. Taking advantage of this interest, the product development people amplified their departure from equilibrium even more by finding out what these eager customers wanted in a PC. The result was their development of the best-selling personal computer, the PC-8000.

APPROPRIATE FAR-FROM-EQUILIBRIUM CONDITIONS

In order for a system to change according to the model of self-organization, specific far-from-equilibrium conditions must develop to unlock the specific type of nonlinearity in that system. There must be a match between nonlinearity and far-from-equilibrium conditions. Efforts to effect change don't succeed if the resulting far-from-equilibrium conditions do not affect the specific kind of nonlinearity in that system.

Studies show, for example, that heat is the only far-from-equilibrium condition that activates the Benard system's nonlinearity and brings about self-organization in the liquid. Other liquids, however, are characterized by different nonlinear relationships among their elements and require different far-from-equilibrium conditions to release their nonlinearity. For example, certain other liquids require pressure as the far-from-equilibrium condition that prompts self-organization.[5]

The necessity for matching nonlinearity with far-from-equilibrium conditions can be seen in another startling example of self-organization: chemical clocks which are marked by the spontaneous, periodic rhythm of colors and shapes.[6] For example, the liquid in a certain kind of chemical clock is red for a period of time, then it becomes blue for another definite period of time, and then it spontaneously becomes red again, and so on. As in the Benard system, specific far-from-equilibrium conditions mobilize the inherent nonlinearity of chemical clocks and thereby prompt self-organization in them. In one type of chemical clock, the far-from-equilibrium conditions are generated both by stirring the mixture and by continually removing certain chemical compounds from the reaction.

Organizations contain various types of nonlinearities that a change agent must match with an appropriate intervention. It is certainly not uncommon for change agents to discover that where one intervention seems to have no effect, another one seems to do the trick and sparks a release of enthusiasm, creativity, and even spontaneous restructuring. Let's see how such a match eventually was found at "Northeast Bay Medical Center."

Matching the Intervention at "Northeast Bay Medical Center"

At "Northeast Bay Medical Center," a system of two hospitals composed of a 500-bed general hospital and an 80-bed specialty hospital, the new president had heard a lot of grumbling about how management didn't care about employees' ideas for improving work-flow methods, rescheduling, using different equipment, ordering less expensive materials, and so on. The president decided to remedy this situation first by having the Human Resources Department conduct an employee attitude survey. Among the findings in the survey was a discrepancy between how employees and their supervisors rated supervisors' listening skills. The employees gave their supervisor's an "F," whereas the supervisors rated themselves an "A" in their ability to listen to employees. Believing this was the problem underlying the grumbling, the president directed Human Resources to set up a management training program in listening skills.

Even though all supervisors and managers attended the program, the president continued to hear the same complaints about lack of employee input. It was clear that something besides improved listening skills was needed. The intervention didn't match the system's nonlinearity. Of course, it is not uncommon for change agents to find that their interventions don't work. What is offered here is a new way to understand *why* these interventions don't work.

"Northeast Bay Medical Center" was a system with an unrewarding and nonparticipative culture. It needed to activate the deeply rooted impulse of employees to participate in decisions related to the functioning of the organization. This had never been permitted in the authoritarian climate the president had inherited. There were no rewards for participating. Management never asked employees for input and if someone did come forth with an idea, management did not act on it. Also, there were no mechanisms for employee involvement. Their suggestion system was particularly ineffective. There were one or two suggestions every couple of months for which the suggester received a coffee mug.

Eventually, the far-from-equilibrium conditions necessary to spark the changes were generated by a set of interventions: the establishment of a productivity improvement incentive plan, which was largely unheard of in the health care environment; extensive training on all levels in how to reward employee participation; a new suggestion system, in which not only the suggesters, but the implementers as well, received substantial cash awards; and the creation of interdepartmental productivity project teams. Each of these interventions was a notable departure from the entrenched equilibrium that had marked the hospitals for years. There also had to be ways that these departures from equilibrium could be propagated throughout the system. This was the challenge faced by the president and the other change agents.

FIRM BUT PERMEABLE BOUNDARIES

Self-organization takes place only under conditions that provide boundaries to the nonlinear amplifications of departures from equilibrium. The boundaries act like the channels that water moves through in a dam in order to run turbines. They harness the tremendous power of self-organization and direct it toward the purpose of the system. Without boundaries, change in linear systems would result in a state of unbridled turbulence.[7] For example, in the Benard system the container acts as a boundary distinguishing the liquid from the environment and protecting the system from environmental variations. This protective function is similar to the use of wetsuits that surfers wear to protect them from cold water. In the Benard system, this function of the container as boundary is particularly obvious given the propensity of a liquid to leak and spread out.

The boundary must be firm and nonpermeable enough to keep the system intact as a unique system. Paradoxically, however, the boundary also must be permeable enough to allow nonlinear conditions from the environment (in this case, heat) to affect the system. The boundaries of the Benard system allow it to take advantage of nonlinear mutual influence, to more effectively transfer heat throughout the liquid. Once the system "discovers" that it can more effectively bridge the internal gaps of temperature and density by using the nonlinear Benard cells rather than the mere linear spread of heat, it does not need to amplify the currents beyond what is necessary. In this way the boundaries contain the internal process.

During self-organization the Benard system can no longer be considered an isolated system since the boundary has been traversed. The system is now in vital connection to its environment—heat from the environment challenges the liquid to come up with a better method of heat transfer. The system in its far-from-equilibrium condition is connected to its variable environment.

With regard to self-organization in human systems, the two aspects of an organization's or work group's boundaries are also necessary: the boundaries must be firm enough to contain the process of self-organization yet permeable enough to allow vital exchange with the environment. Let's see how this was managed in the case of weak boundaries that resulted from the merger of two companies with equally strong organizational cultures.

Boundary work at "Pearl and Pebble Records"

When "Pearl and Pebble Records," a leader in the recording industry, bought and merged two smaller record producers, each with an established reputation in a different aspect of the business, it faced a big problem. The two companies had simply been absorbed into "P&P." A few of the departments from the acquired companies retained their separate status as they had already existed as such in the smaller companies, but the rest of the departments were heaped together into the corresponding larger department of the parent company.

The hope was that a melding would occur as the new personnel worked together on common projects. Even though "P&P" was now in a position to produce records for a much wider audience, the strong and distinctive organizational cultures of both companies were proving to be an obstacle to cooperation between the employees from the two companies. The newly combined departments now had weak and ambiguous boundaries, for it was unclear who reported to whom, who in the department was to act as liaison with other departments, and so on.

After nearly eight months this situation had grown worse as one company became dominant and subsumed the other by winning a series of important corporate battles in the boardroom. Senior management at "P&P" decided that formal intervention was necessary and hired a consulting company to expedite an organizational change.

Team-building sessions were set up to firm the boundaries of the departments: participants negotiated and clarified roles, redefined responsibilities, and developed team missions. Once they strengthened departmental boundaries, participants could proceed with the next phase of interdepartmental team-building: forging a vital connection between newly formed departments. We can see here the twofold process of boundary work required to support self-organization: firming and traversing boundaries. Chapter 7 details boundary work.

UNPREDICTABLE OUTCOMES

Self-organization is a process in which chance plays an important role in the change process. Events take place and structures emerge that cannot be anticipated. For example, the self-organizing Benard cells may rotate clockwise or counterclockwise depending on the amplification of initially random currents (see Figure 3-3). This randomness makes it impossible to predict the direction of the rotation before the onset of self-organization.

The role of chance relates to the unpredictability of outcomes associated with nonlinearity that we explored in the last chapter. Events take place and structures emerge that cannot be anticipated. Nonlinear

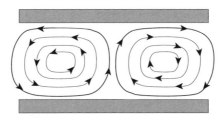

Figure 3-3. Self-Organizing Currents

Source: Adapted from Gregoire Nicolis, "Physics of Far-from-Equilibrium Systems and Self-Organization." In Paul Davies, ed., *The New Physics* (Cambridge: Cambridge Univ. Press), p. 318

science has clearly shown that the evolution of a nonlinear system quickly surpasses any predictions of the system's behavior based on an assessment of its initial status. This makes the dynamics of change into a process that is evolutionary, organic, and serendipitous.

This also means the role and function of planning in the change process must be reconsidered. Planning can no longer be regarded as an activity whose success depends on accurate assessments of the current status of the organization, nor as a precise predictive tool, nor as something that takes place only before an intervention. In the self-organization model, planning is conceived as a continuing adjustment of the change strategy with the changing conditions. Assessment of the organization is not abandoned, but it becomes an ongoing process of comparing the present state of the system with its previous states.[8] Planning has gone from being a future-directed activity to now including an important backward-looking component. Furthermore, the tools of prediction based on a linear view of systems are being replaced by

Characteristics of Self-Organization

- Spontaneous and radical reorganizing
- Activating nonlinearity
- Interrupting equilibrium-seeking tendencies
- Using departures from equilibrium
- Matching far-from-equilibrium conditions to nonlinearity
- Establishing firm but permeable boundaries
- Generating unpredictable outcomes

all the new methods of nonlinear science (development in this area is beginning to find ways in which these nonlinear methods can be applied to organizations).

In general, the new role of planning in the self-organization model is quite similar to the process of *action research* as originally developed by Kurt Lewin.[9] Action research emphasizes a cycle of action, feedback, and response to the feedback as the rhythm of organizational change. In a sense, the planner becomes an explorer and a discoverer, and it must be recognized that the latter roles demand a different set of skills than those of the accurate predictor.

4

FROM RESISTANCE TO ATTRACTION

The softest of stuff in the world
Penetrates quickly the hardest;
Insubstantial, it enters
Where no room is.
—TAO TE CHING (VERSE 43)

Sooner or later, proponents of organizational change probably find themselves up against the question: How can resistance be overcome? Often, the intensity of the resistance can lead change agents to abandon their original intentions. Here is a typical sequence to the change process: change agents initiate a change; employees respond less-than-whole-heartedly; the promoters of change see the employee response as resistance to change, then focus on how to overcome this resistance.

New research into nonlinear systems challenges the concept that resistance to change is inherent to systems. The traditional conception, in fact, is turned on its head—in nonlinear systems resistance shifts from being an inherent property to being a temporary condition of a system currently at equilibrium. Likewise, change shifts from the result of an external pressure to become a primary, inherent property of a system. In other words, the tendency toward change becomes the basic property of a system, while resistance recedes into secondary and temporary importance.

In this chapter, we take a closer look at resistance to change in order to reinterpret it in the light of the new model of change. First, we'll look at an example of resistance to change. Then, we'll see how employees response to change is viewed more effectively as an *attraction* to positive values rather than a negatively conceived opposition to change. We shall see that resistance is better understood as *attraction*.

RESISTANCE TO CHANGE AT "PARKSIDE HOSPITAL"

At a large urban teaching hospital, "Parkside Hospital," bed occupancy rates were declining due to competition.[1] Top management implemented a "guest-relations" program to upgrade the quality of interaction between front-line employees, patients, and their families. The first employees targeted for this courtesy skills program were the floor secretaries, who acted as the hub on each nursing unit. They were responsible for such tasks as ordering lab tests, filling out paperwork, answering questions from family members, relaying phone calls, providing information about bed availability, and so on. This group was targeted because they had a reputation for being abrupt, snappy, and even nasty in their interactions with patients, relatives, and staff.

At the first session, the instructor of the courtesy program had to pass through the participants as they congregated in the hall outside the classroom, glowering at him as he walked up to the door. The door was locked and no one had seen fit to call security to get a key. Once a key was finally produced and the session got under way, this lackluster response turned to outright hostility: "We know how to do our jobs—it's our supervisors who don't!" to "You don't know what it's like dealing with these patients!" to "Who are you to tell us what to do?"

Later, the "Parkside" managers who were spearheading the program made a typical move—they labeled the employees' hostile response as resistance to change. This label consequently limited their strategies to either overpowering resistance by a greater appeal to authority or subduing it through persuasion. Thus, one top manager exclaimed, "They just don't have a choice! They have to attend!" Whereas another executive said, "We simply must do a better job of selling the benefits of this program."

Labeling resistance turns the organizational change process into a clash of wills. Again, we have the donkey model of change described in Chapter 1. On the one hand, individual employees are viewed as donkey-like in their stubborn and willful resistance to change. On the other hand, work units and organizations are seen as sluggish, systemic masses mired in inertia. Change, then, becomes a matter of imposition and opposition, the change agent having to be a powerful enough steam locomotive to get the train moving!

THE AFFIRMATIVE CORE OF RESISTANCE

The imposition/opposition dynamic is a common experience of managers and change agents. To be sure, the donkey model often accurately reflects the pervasive phenomenon of resistance to organizational change. After all, organizations and work groups rarely go along cheerfully with a change project.

The problem, however, lies in the ramifications that arise from the label resistance. Resistance, with its underlying donkey connotations, conjures up a picture of employees as obstinate, stubborn, and willfully oppositional. Coming up with appropriate responses to this picture of resistance is severely constrained to strategies that overpower, overcome, or outmatch the resistance.

The field of psychotherapy is one place where these pictures of resistance and the accompanying strategies to overcome it have been thoroughly studied. Everyday in their offices, counselors and psychotherapists of all persuasions face the phenomena of change and resistance on the part of their clients. Clients are seeking change in their careers, their relationships with families and friends, or their self-defeating behavior, attitudes, thought processes, and habitual emotional responses. But, as in the case of organizational change, as soon as a change is initiated something that looks like resistance occurs.

Yet, recent research had yielded insights in the fields of counseling and psychotherapy that conclude that resistance is more than a donkey-like, stubborn opposition to change. Instead, a client resists change when the change is perceived as a threat to the client's sense of autonomy, integrity, and even ideals.[2] This puts resistance to change in a vastly different context—resistance becomes the best way of surviving that a client currently knows. In the face of threatening change, clients are not so much resisting change as being *attracted* to an affirmative core of self-esteem, dignity, and a sense of personal power.

Five salient features emerge from this reinterpretation of resistance that can be applied to the phenomenon of resistance to organizational change:

- Resistance indicates that change is perceived as a threat to a currently held and largely unconscious belief system.

- Resistance is largely unconscious; therefore, it can't be dismissed as conscious obstinacy.

- Resistance is an expected and crucial element in the change process and, as such, is a sign of progress, not failure.

- Resistance is an attraction to an affirmative core that involves the need to survive with dignity, autonomy, and integrity.

- Resistance needs to be approached with respect and empathy.

In an organization, resistance reflects employees' needs to protect their sense of dignity, integrity, or ideals rather than their supposed primal inclinations to inertia. This need may be largely unconscious, and therefore, may appear as willful obstinacy. Trying to overpower this resistance, then, is counterproductive in the long run because strategies of force are tantamount to threatening the dignity and integrity of the individuals involved.

FROM RESISTORS TO ATTRACTORS

Fortunately, understanding organizational change as a process of self-organization provides a role for resistance without permitting it to

The Affirmative Core of Resistance at "Falcon Computers"

Interpreting resistance as attraction can be seen in how employees at "Falcon Computers" in Silicon Valley resisted an attempt to change the corporate culture.[3] Founded six years ago, "Falcon" initially went through a huge growth spurt, but then a year ago the ceiling seemed to have been reached—sales plateaued and fierce competition began gaining the upper hand. After several months of stagnation, top management came to the conclusion that "Falcon" needed to transform its organizational culture in order to become more open and participative which hopefully would stimulate higher productivity.

The president and vice presidents of "Falcon Computers" met regularly with external consultants to develop a blueprint of the new culture—Falcon Values. The new document described the proper attitude to be taken with customers: quality was highlighted (zero-defect products), preferred communication style would be open, and managers would use participative decision-making methods. Falcon Values was distributed to middle managers who were enjoined to meet in closed sessions to discuss and further refine it. At culture meetings, where the top executives discussed the culture documents, the seating was arranged in a circle to reflect the new more participative and egalitarian culture.

While the culture change endeavor was underway, however, "Falcon" went about its business according to the corporate culture that had been in place since the early days. The president and vice-presidents met, made their top-level decisions behind closed doors, and kept the results of their decisions close to the vest. Because both cash-flow and inventory were overloaded, computers known to be defective were nevertheless still being sent to customers. The head of security incorporated the new values into the old by deciding employee security badges should only include first names.

As you might have guessed, the attempted change of corporate culture at "Falcon" didn't succeed. The employees resisted the change. After all, the culture that actually influenced behavior was the firmly ensconced managerial hierarchy, the closed nature of managerial decision-making, and the priority of making quick cash over the quality of product. This underlying set of organizational beliefs was attracting the employees' behavior since it was only by following these old ways and resisting the new ways that an employee's real survival hinged.

entirely characterize a system's potential. In the new model, resistance is merely an initial and temporary attractor of the long-range developmental trajectory of a nonlinear system. Chapter 2 described nonlinear systems, which evolve into regions of more and more complex attractors so that the potential for growth in the system is not limited to any one particular attractor regime. It is only at equilibrium conditions, where linear processes predominate, that resistance to change governs a system. As such, resistance simply indicates that the organizational patterns that are operating are initially and temporarily *attracting* the system to remain the way it is.

Change is a matter of transiting into new attractors, a process brought about by appropriate far-from-equilibrium conditions. This implies that change does not overcome resistance, but that resistance is expected, accepted, and respected. Resistance ceases to be an issue when it is no longer the dominant attractor of a system. That this is more than a semantical shift in the meaning of resistance will become clearer later in this chapter and in the next chapter as we further explore those organizational patterns that initially attract the system and lead to the phenomenon of resistance.

The new model moves the issue away from how or what a system resists to how and to what a system is attracted. To appreciate this new role for resistance, the concept of attractors must be explored in greater depth.

The concept of attractor originated by looking at the long-term behavior of systems. It was discovered that the behavior of the systems studied settled into regular and predictable patterns when the system was in the region of a particular phase of its long-term evolution. These phases were termed *attractors* since they attracted the behavior of a system to stay within the specific pattern congruent with each of the attractors.

These phases, or transitions, through more and more complex attractor regimes, are analogous to the developmental stages of a person's life. Each stage of development has clearly recognizable features: infancy and the clumsy exploration of new behaviors; childhood and complex learning of self-responsibility as well as cooperating with others; puberty and the disturbing awakening of new desires, and so on through adolescence, young adulthood, mid-life crises, and old age. At each stage of life, certain patterns of behavior and emotions resonate with the issues that confront the person.

Similarly, an attractor is a pattern that defines the behavior of a system when it is in a particular phase of development. In a particular attractor regime, the functioning of the system is limited to what is congruent with a particular attractor. That is, the attractor represents how the system is organized to accomplish the tasks that are operative in that particular phase of development. In a particular attractor regime, a system's behavior may temporarily be perturbed out of its normal behavior, but the system will eventually settle back into the prescribed behavior allowed by the attractor.

A CHILD'S SWING: A SHIFT IN ATTRACTORS

To appreciate how the concept of an attractor captures the eventual behavior of a system, consider the movement of a swing. At first the swing is probably hanging fairly motionless, except perhaps for an occasional breeze. Placing a child on the seat and merely pulling the swing back and letting it go only causes the swing to go back and forth for a little while. The swing eventually slows down and returns to its original motionless position. The attractor of this simple swing system is the original motionless hanging, technically called a *fixed-point attractor* (since on a graph a point is used to indicate the position of rest). This attractor represents the fact that the swing, even if temporarily disturbed out of its initial equilibrium by pulling or pushing, eventually settles back into the vertical position. Thus, the long-term behavior of the swing ultimately is determined by its return to a state of rest, or equilibrium. All that an initial push or pull can do is temporarily perturb the system to start the swinging motion. Eventually, due to gravity, the system settles back to its initial pattern of rest. The swing is not so much resisting an initial push as it is being attracted to its favored position of rest.

If that was all there was to swings, however, they would be no fun at all! The whole point of swings is that you can make them continue to swing and even increase the arc. Children (and adults) get a thrill not from a swing that eventually stops under the sway of a fixed point attractor, but by doing something that either keeps the swinging movement or makes the swing go even higher. This can be done either by shifting one's weight in sync with the direction of the swinging or by someone behind the swing giving it an extra push each time the swing comes back.

In both cases, the swing keeps going rather than returning to its initial state of rest. Therefore, the second example is very different from the first example where the swinging simply stopped. That is, the behavior of the swing is no longer defined by a fixed-point attractor. Instead, the attractor of continually swinging back and forth is called a *limit-cycle attractor* (limit cycle is a way of characterizing, on a graph, the continual back-and-forth movement of the swing when it is driven by a push or a shift of weight). As long as the push drives the system, the system is attracted to behavior that is consonant with the limit-cycle attractor that keeps it swinging.

The limit-cycle attractor of the continual swinging is similar to the attractor at work in the case of a metronome, which goes back and forth at regular periods to help music students practice beats. Another example is the nonlinear system of schnauzers and mice described in Chapter 2 in which a circular pattern on a graph shows the constraints on the overall behavior of the populations of schnauzers and mice together in a physical arena. This attractor defines the pattern of relationship between the schnauzers and mice, which is characterized by interdependent changes in the population of schnauzers and mice.

The swing system shifts from the initial-point attractor of motionless hanging to the limit-cycle attractor of the swing that is driven, as a result of a far-from-equilibrium condition. In this case, the far-from-equilibrium condition is generated either by a periodic push on the swing or by the person on the swing shifting his or her weight. The far-from-equilibrium condition causes the system to transit into a new attractor regime, so that the behavior of the driven swing is far different from the behavior of a swing that gently returns to rest after an initial push.

ATTRACTOR AS CONTEXT OF A SYSTEM

An attractor defines the context of a system's functioning at each demarcated phase of its evolution. It determines what is possible as well as what is impossible within the system at that particular phase. The distinction between context and content clearly shows how attractors define the context of a system's behavior.

For example, consider a simple system composed of a room with a thermostat that regulates the temperature within a comfortable range. The thermostat senses when the temperature varies too far above or below a pre-set range and sends a message to turn the air conditioning off or on, depending on the temperature in the room.

In this simple system, the *context* is defined as the set range that determines the possibilities for the temperature. This setting is the context defining the limits of behavior of the room's temperature. *Content*, however, is defined as the actual temperature in the room that the thermostat senses. To change this content, one could open the windows, turn a space heater on, pull the drapes on a sunny day, and so on. The content of the temperature can change.

All these changes of content only change the temperature temporarily. If the thermostat is in working order, changes in content that go beyond the defined preset range eventually are eliminated by the action of the thermostat.

The preset range and the action of the thermostat are analogous to an attractor of a system. The attractor defines the context that constrains the behavior of the system. Content can change, but only within the limits set by the context. To change the content permanently requires a change in the context; that is, a shift in the attractor. A shift in attractors changes the qualitative behavior of the system; for example, in Chapter 3 the Benard liquid undergoing self-organization represents a shift in the system to a new attractor regime.

RESISTANCE AS AN ATTRACTOR UNDER
EQUILIBRIUM CONDITIONS

Before the onset of self-organization in the Benard system, equilibrium conditions dominate the liquid. Under equilibrium conditions, the system maintains its current means of functioning and does not allow any kind of disturbance to change its current pattern permanently. The state of unchanging equilibrium lasts as long as the linear method of heat conduction is effective in coping with the warming of the liquid. In other words, the Benard liquid resists the change in both its structure and its means of heat conduction. *An equilibrium condition where linear processes predominate is equivalent to a system's resistance to change.*

As nonlinear systems undergo transformation, however, they pass through more and more complex regimes of attractors. If the qualitative behavior of the system is not changing, then the attractor that defines the context of the system's behavior is not changing. This evolutionary view of system change, when applied to work groups and organizations, leads one to conclude that resistance to change is merely an initial attractor in the long-range developmental thrust of the organization or work group.

Resistance to change in an organization or work group, then, is a sign that the organization or work group is at a phase in its development in which it is attracted to behaviors that only appear to be behaviors of resistance. Actually, the behaviors are congruent with what is possible at that phase in the group's development. When a work group or organization is supposedly resisting change, the system is merely in an equilibrium condition. But what exactly is this equilibrium and where does it derive its power to attract the system?

What is possible?

SYSTEMS SEEKING EQUILIBRIUM

Instead of children on swings, this time imagine children on a seesaw bobbing up and down, seeking to balance and then upset the balance of the seesaw. In ancient Greek thought, a similar balanced state of a lever on a fulcrum was called *equilibrium.* Much thought went into figuring out how to achieve equilibrium with different weights and distances between the weights on the lever.

If someone places weights in the right positions on the lever and balances them, and then the system is disturbed out of balance by a temporary push, the lever bobs up and down until it comes to rest again in a state of equilibrium. In this sense, the lever system seeks to return to its original state of undisturbed equilibrium whenever it is disturbed out of that state.

Thus, it could be said that when the lever is balanced, this state of balance becomes the *equilibrium attractor* that determines the long-run behavior of the system even when it is disturbed. In fact, if the equilibrium attractor dominates the system, any attempt to change the system from its state of balance will fail in the long run, for the system will strive to return to its original state of balance. In this sense, resistance to change simply indicates that the system is under the thrall of an equilibrium attractor.

This is why equilibrium-seeking has played such an important role in understanding the stability and order of work groups or organizations. Thus, Lewin relied on the idea that systems seek equilibrium when he developed his famous force-field analysis of organizations (see Figure 4-1). For example, the recalcitrance of a factory work unit in the face of various attempts to change its productivity standard could be understood as an equilibrium-seeking force field between the forces that push for change and the forces that resist change.

What if, instead, this recalcitrance of the factory work unit indicates the temporary dominance of the attractor that rules the system when it is at equilibrium. That would mean this resistance is merely an initial phase of the work group's evolutionary potential, a potential that becomes actualized when the group is in a far-from-equilibrium condition. But what is it that makes up the attracting power of this initial

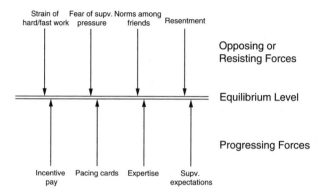

Figure 4-1. Lewin's Equilibrium Force-Field

Equilibrium-Seeking at "Wall Street Stocks and Bonds"

The tendency of a work unit to restore its equilibrium can be seen by what happened to the word-processing pool at "Wall Street Stocks and Bonds," a large financial services company. The manager became concerned that productivity was falling behind the projected standards for the current quarter. After trying different remedies such as changing schedules and task assignments, the manager brought in a job-design specialist who concluded the seating arrangement was to blame. Because the work stations were laid out in rows, with each station next to the other, the computer operators could talk with the operator right next to them. All this talking was surely interfering with productivity.

The remedy? Stagger the work stations so that there would be an empty space next to each operator—no one to talk to! Therefore, maintenance came in and rearranged the work area. The result? Productivity declined even further, absenteeism went up, and the word processors were spending more time at the coffee cart, water fountain, and bathroom. The number of complaints about sore backs and necks soared since the operators now had to cock their heads to the side and back to talk to their staggered neighbors.

The manager was perplexed by what she saw as resistance to change. She had to admit that things were worse than they were before the change. Not being able to come up with a further remedy to this worsened state, the manager eventually settled on restoring the rows to the original arrangement. She had to find other solutions to the productivity problem.

tion. But what is it that makes up the attracting power of this initial equilibrium attractor?

KEEPERS OF EQUILIBRIUM

When a particular attractor regime dominates a system, certain processes maintain the attractive power of the attractor. That is, certain processes in the system work to limit what's allowed to take place in the system within a circumscribed range of behavior.

In the analogy of the thermostat, the attractor is the set range of temperatures. In the thermostat, the power of attraction is a result of various processes: the process that establishes the present equilibrium (the preset range of temperatures); the process that senses when the system threatens to depart from equilibrium (a thermometer and device for flagging temperature extremes outside the preset range); and the process that activates the system to return equilibrium (turning the air conditioner on or off). In other words, the power of the equilibrium attractor is the result of equilibrium-seeking processes in the system that are activated when the system threatens to depart from equilibrium. As long as the equilibrium attractor dominates the system, equilibrium-seeking processes are at work in the system maintaining the equilibrium.

When we apply the self-organization model to human organizations and work groups, resistance can be seen as a manifestation of an equilibrium attractor. That is, resistance indicates that a work group or organization is under the sway of an equilibrium attractor, which invites an exploration of the equilibrium-seeking processes that occur in a work group or organization.

Equilibrium-seeking processes maintain equilibrium by eliminating any departures from the current status of the work group or organization. Following the attractor, they keep the behavior of the system within the accepted setting, or culture, of the group by disallowing deviations from behavioral norms, decision-making methods, work design, managerial styles, and so on. In an equilibrium-seeking organization, a manager's job is to control and dampen variances, for example, budget variances, work performance variances, and inventory variances and to keep the unpredictable to a bare minimum. The emphasis on planning, prediction, accurate anticipation, and control is the basis of the whole edifice of planned change that has guided organizational change interventions thus far.

Equilibrium-seeking processes insure that all of the behavior in the system conforms to the attractor. They keep the system isolated from environmental variations that threaten to change the system's operation, and they keep any creative impulse toward new behaviors in check. They mask nonlinear growth potential in the system so that the system appears to be a linear process. Furthermore, equilibrium-seeking processes strive to keep new information out of the system because it has the potential to disrupt current operations. In other words, equilibrium-seeking processes serve to maintain stability at all costs.

A primary culprit for equilibrium-seeking processes in work groups and organizations is the self-fulfilling prophecy. That is, the beliefs and expectations of managers lead to actions on the part of employees, which, in turn, lead to results that confirm the original beliefs and expectations of the manager. Chapter 5 goes into much greater detail about self-fulfilling prophecies and how they point to the essential nonlinearity of organizations. For now, all that needs to be emphasized is that a self-fulfilling prophecy is a self-reinforcing interaction of belief and behavior that leads an organization into an information-tight insularity, dominates the work unit, and leads to an equilibrium-seeking state. In other words, the circular interaction at the heart of a self-fulfilling prophecy serves to resist change.

Resistance as Attraction

- Resistance to change signifies that an organization is under the sway of an equilibrium attractor.

- An equilibrium attractor maintains its hegemony by equilibrium-seeking processes.

- Resistance to change is a way of labeling the equilibrium-seeking processes in a work group or organization.

- Resistance to change is a result of self-fulfilling prophecies in an organization or work group.

MOVING BEYOND RESISTANCE: TRANSITION TO A NEW ATTRACTOR

The self-fulfilling prophecy is the mechanism that keeps an organization under the spell of an equilibrium attractor. Transformation occurs when the equilibrium-seeking tendency of the self-fulfilling prophecy is disrupted. This is not a matter of overcoming resistance. Resistance is only a sign of the system's attraction to the equilibrium attraction. Disrupting equilibrium-seeking processes requires far-from-equilibrium conditions.

The idea of nonlinear systems passing through various attractor regimes is one of the startling discoveries of the new science of chaos and far-from-equilibrium thermodynamics. Indeed, self-organization represents the nonlinear transition from one attractor to another. The emergence of the new attractor signifies the onset of self-organization.

Let's look again at the transformation of the Benard liquid. Equilibrium conditions in the Benard liquid exist when it operates as a system isolated from its environment and is in a state of comparative rest and sameness. Equilibrium, however, is only an initial phase of this system's transformation since far-from-equilibrium conditions can induce the system to transit to new attractor regimes, in which self-organization changes the inherent dynamics of the system. Therefore, a system need not be confined to its equilibrium phase, which is only one phase in the evolution of increasing complexity. A system that goes beyond equilibrium has the potential to pass into other regions of attractors that represent new dynamic possibilities for the system. Therefore, equilibrium is not the only state a system seeks or attracts: It is only one phase of a much more complex trajectory of a system.

Similarly, resistance to change is merely the initial response of a work group or organization to change. This resistance dominates the system as long as the far-from-equilibrium conditions do not activate the system's inherent nonlinear potential for growth. The so-called resistance to change disappears when the system self-organizes.

In the traditional model of organizational change all organizational systems are characterized by an innate tendency to seek equilibrium and oppose change. Organizational change efforts must struggle against this innate inclination. Furthermore, when change does occur, it is considered the result of imposing an external force that disturbs the equilibrium and leads to a corresponding shift in equilibrium levels. In this kind of change, there is no possibility for novelty in the system, for novelty indicates that the system is functioning in a new way. This new manner of functioning has no place in the simple equilibrium force-field picture of change. In fact, equilibrium-based models cannot account for change, growth, or development.[4]

In the self-organization model of system change, the tendency to change and develop is inherent in the system's very possibilities; therefore, resistance to change does not need an external force to get it moving, as in the donkey model of change. The self-organization model requires that the focus shift away from anticipating, dislodging, and overcoming resistance to discovering the equilibrium attractors and the far-from-equilibrium conditions that can spark a transition to new, more complex attractors. Ultimately, nonlinear systems, including organizations and work groups, do not seek equilibrium; they seek to evolve, a fundamental potential of their complex nonlinearity.

An advantage to shifting the frame of reference from resistance to attraction is that it lifts the whole context of organizational change out of the arena of contending forces. Looking at equilibrium-seeking as a matter not of resistance, but of attraction, opens up the possibility that organizational systems don't just seek to oppose change; rather, work groups and organizations seek to develop and evolve.

Resistance is just a way of talking about how the system has to behave in a manner consonant with the attractor. Actually, the system does not resist anything, it is attracted to its attractor. This does not mean, of course, that it is impossible for systems to change. It means, instead, that real transformation consists of a change in attractors. This type of change is brought about by far-from-equilibrium conditions.

Transformation consists of transiting to a new attractor, which changes the context of the system's functioning. Changes in context then, signify a transition out of the equilibrium attractor altogether and into more complex attractors. Transition to new attractors is already an inherent potential of the nonlinearity of the system and is brought about by far-from-equilibrium conditions.

The next chapter explores in greater depth how self-fulfilling prophecies serve to maintain equilibrium in a work unit or organization. Later chapters discuss how far-from-equilibrium conditions can be generated to result in a process of transformation.

THE EQUILIBRIUM EFFECT OF SELF-FULFILLING PROPHECIES

Cease striving, then there will be transformation.
—CHUANG TZU (BOOK 11)

Promoters of change seldom encounter organizations that are eager to change; most often they confront resistance to change. The new nonlinear model of change, however, sees systems as inherently seeking change.

This apparent discrepancy is resolved when the concept of resistance to change is reevaluated in the new model of nonlinear systems. The new model doesn't deny the phenomenon of resistance, but it does challenge two assumptions that underlie the traditional concept of resistance. First, the new model questions whether the term *resistance* is particularly useful for understanding employees' usual response to organizational change. As we saw in the last chapter, the connotations of resistance lead directly to the donkey model of change and the concomitant restricted range of strategies that are available to change agents.

Second, instead of seeing resistance as basic and change as an imposition, the new model encompasses resistance by seeing it as merely an initial, temporary attractor *when a system is at equilibrium.* Under equilibrium conditions, patterns that operate in a system attract the system to stay the way it is. At equilibrium, these patterns dominate the system and cover up the system's inherent nonlinear power to change. Thus, the system appears linear and acts in a linear fashion. When a system transits to far-from-equilibrium conditions that interrupt equilibrium-seeking processes, however, the new conditions unleash the innate nonlinear potential for change and resistance no longer attracts the system.

What we need to understand at this juncture are those organizational dynamics that keep a system at equilibrium and hold its nonlinear growth potential at bay. That is, we need to understand what makes the essentially nonlinear system of a work group or organization behave in a linear fashion.

ORGANIZATIONS AS NONLINEAR SYSTEMS

In 1988, a series of mishaps plagued Delta Airlines after many years of trouble-free service. It started when shortly after takeoff a plane on a flight from Los Angeles to Cincinnati suddenly lost altitude and the crew warned the passengers to prepare for a crash landing in the Pacific. Fortunately, one of the pilots realized he had inadvertently turned off the engines after takeoff and instantly turned them back on. The plane gained altitude and continued on to Cincinnati.

This event, however, was just the first of many misadventures at Delta: planes landed at the wrong airports; all manner of technical difficulties afflicted the airline; and several near misses occurred in the air and on the ground. Surprisingly, all these mishaps happened within a few days of each other. It was as if the first misfortune jinxed the airline and started an escalating trend. The FAA concluded human error united the episodes, but how did human error amplify in such an alarming fashion?

VICIOUS CIRCLES: THE SELF-FULFILLING PROPHECY
AS A NONLINEAR SYSTEM

Michael Corey sees, in the epidemic of mistakes at Delta, evidence of a *self-fulfilling prophecy* that contaminated the operation of the airline.[1] In this self-fulfilling prophecy, an inordinate fear of making a mistake led to a state of mind in which mistakes were more likely to be made. The initial mistake united with inordinate fear trigged a trend of mistakes, a nonlinear disproportion, since a small event precipitated a whole slew of related events.

A run on a bank is a typical example of a self-fulfilling prophecy: Fear that their bank is going under leads frantic depositors to withdraw their funds. This run on withdrawals seriously compromises the bank's finances, and the catastrophic downturn in the bank's financial condition confirms the original fears of bank failure. As a result, runs on the bank escalate and, finally, the bank does indeed collapse. The original fearful *prophecy* that the bank will collapse is fulfilled by the very actions spurred on by the prophecy—hence the term: self-fulfilling prophecy.

The structure of the self-fulfilling prophecy consists of an initial expectation (belief, assumption, or attitude) that leads to behaviors that result in a condition that confirms the original expectation (see Figure 5-1).

At the heart of the escalating structure of the self-fulfilling prophecy is the nonlinear, multidirectional, and mutual influence discussed in Chapter 2. The original expectations, the ensuing actions, and the confirming results mutually influence each other. The original expectations influence the actions, and the actions lead to an outcome which, in turn,

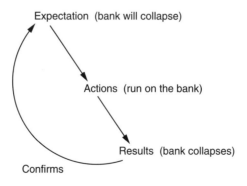

Figure 5-1. The Self-Fulfilling Prophecy

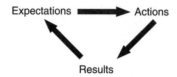

Figure 5-2. The Nonlinear Structure of the Self-Fulfilling Prophecy

influences the original expectations. As the actions increase in frequency, the original expectation is strengthened, and as the original expectation is strengthened, there is an even further increase in actions in an ever-increasing, nonlinear cycle (see Figure 5-2).

It is crucial to recognize that in the dynamics of a self-fulfilling prophecy, the presence of an element leads to an intensification of this very element.[2] In the case of the run on a bank, the element that intensifies is the fear that the bank will fail. This fear leads to actions that intensify the fear, and on and on in a vicious circle. Because of the nonlinear nature of this circular interaction, the original expectation needs only enough initial credibility to start the ball rolling. Actions then lead to outcomes that heighten the original expectation. That is why a weak initial belief can lead to a huge nonlinear effect.

SELF-FULFILLING PROPHECIES MAINTAIN EQUILIBRIUM AND RESIST CHANGE

Self-Fulfilling Prophecies Are Self-Confirming

The nonlinear, circular structure of the self-fulfilling prophecies keeps an organizational system at equilibrium. This nonlinear cycle creates a barrier around work groups and organizations that keeps them isolated and closed-off to new information or news ways of interacting with their environments. The self-fulfilling prophecy has the power to do this because it is *self-confirming*—its own beliefs reinforce themselves by way of actions congruent with those beliefs. Therefore, it doesn't need any information outside its own insular structure to keep it going. The circular and closed interaction between beliefs and behaviors dominates the dynamics of the system.

For example, the fear that the bank is failing is self-confirming since it leads to behaviors that bring about the failure. Even giving these depositors financial statements that show to the contrary, for example, that the bank is in sound financial condition, the new information would probably not be accepted or lead to a change in behavior. The persons caught up in this self-fulfilling prophecy simply are not open to new information or changes in the structure. Their beliefs are reinforced when they see others who, caught-up in the same self-fulfilling prophecy, are also withdrawing their money. Therefore, the self-fulfilling prophecy serves as a barrier to new, disconfirming information, and thereby keeps the persons caught up in the structure of the self-fulfilling prophecy from changing either behavior or their beliefs (see Figure 5-3). In this way the self-fulfilling prophecy resists change in the system. It is like a vortex that sucks in all the available energy of the system in order to maintain itself in its circular, insular pattern. As a result, no energy in the system is available for change.

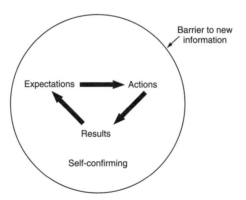

Figure 5-3. The Self-confirming and Isolating Character of the Self-fulfilling Prophecy

Self-Fulfilling Prophecies Block Information

Another example of how a self-fulfilling prophecy resists change by blocking information can be seen in a religious cult that existed in the mid-1950s.[3] The cult's leader announced the world was going to end on a certain day and his followers accordingly prepared for this calamity by selling their homes and gathering in a particular location. The date came along, however, and the world didn't end.

Now, one would have thought the fact the world did not end would be information that challenged and undermined the followers' belief in the leader's credibility and would lead to a change in the behavior of the cult. But, this did not happen. Instead, another belief emerged that justified the original expectation by pointing out a mistake in the eschatological calculations. This enabled the followers and their leader to readdress the issue of when the last day was to occur. Their self-fulfilling prophecy was so strong, the system had become information-proof and change was effectively resisted.

This information-proof cult is not such a far cry from the way many organizations keep vital information from affecting the way they do business. For example, certain typewriter manufacturers did not allow information about the tremendous potential of word processors to interfere with their determination to produce only typewriters.[4] Caught up in a self-fulfilling prophecy they identified with so completely, they prevented themselves from receiving information that disconfirmed these same beliefs. As a result, these firms resisted changing to word processor manufacturing, and many of them, accordingly, went out of business.

By isolating organizations, by keeping new information from entering the system, by reinforcing the original assumptions and norms of the group, self-fulfilling prophecies are organizational equilibrium-seeking processes that maintain the regime of an equilibrium attractor and lead to resistance to change. Just as equilibrium conditions hide the nonlinear potential of a system to transform, self-fulfilling prophecies conceal the growth potential of work groups and organizations. In other words, self-fulfilling prophecies in organizations lead to resistance to change by setting up equilibrium conditions. This resistance, however, is really attraction to the belief system inherent in the self-fulfilling prophecy.

Surviving at "Parkside Hospital." The role of self-fulfilling prophecies in resisting change can be seen in the response of the floor secretaries to the courtesy training program at the "Parkside Hospital" (see Chapter 4). The floor secretaries' position is a low-paying job in a highly stressed work setting. They are not only the hub of the nursing unit, they are the hub of the stress that circulates around the hospital. After all, patients are not hospitalized because they are happy and feel great.

It is mostly an environment of pain and suffering, of trauma and dying. This affects everyone: the patients and their families, the visitors, and the staff.

Moreover, the hierarchy is reinforced by the prestige ensconsed in advanced degrees. Doctors feel entitled to order everyone around, and nurses reflect their experience of diminishment by physicians by the way they treat the floor secretaries. In such an environment, the floor secretaries expect to be treated abruptly and with very little consideration. They then act in a manner congruent with these expectations, which leads the rest of the staff, as well as patients and their families, to confirm that the floor secretaries are indeed a hostile lot. Thus, the abrupt, snappy, and nasty attitudes and behaviors of these employees are their means of survival in a difficult organizational system.

It is easy to see that acting courteously in such an environment could be perceived as a threat to their very survival. Stress is such a central and relentless aspect of their jobs that they resist anything that threatens to make their job even more stressful, which is how the new training program was viewed. The self-fulfilling prophecy behind their discourteous behavior is how they learned to survive. This became their equilibrium attractor, empowered by their need to survive.

The CEO's self-fulfilling prophecy at Johnsonville Foods. Another example of a self-fulfilling prophecy can be seen at Johnsonville Foods, a producer of sausages in Sheboygan, Wisconsin. In the early 1980s, Ralph Stayer, the CEO, initiated a corporatewide change that fell victim to a self-fulfilling prophecy emanating from Stayer's expectations.[5] In 1980 Johnsonville Foods was growing 20 percent annually. Sales were strong, and the quality of sausages high. Stayer realized things were not all that rosy, however. He had a persistent knot in his stomach, employees seemed apathetic and did not take much responsibility for their work, and fierce competition loomed on the horizon.

Stayer concluded Johnsonville Foods needed a drastic change. So he inaugurated the change program: "Acting on instinct, I ordered a change...No one asked for more responsibility, I forced it down their throats." But this imposition of a new participative culture ran head-on against the self-fulfilling prophecy of Stayer's authoritarian leadership style. But as it turned out, this self-fulfilling prophecy was a *virtuous circle* by its ability to generate success. In Stayer's own words:

The business had grown nicely and that very success was my biggest obstacle to change. I had made all the decisions about purchasing, scheduling, quality, pricing, marketing, sales, hiring, and all the rest of it. Now the very things that had brought me success—my centralized control, my aggressive behavior, my authoritarian business practices—were creating the environment that made me so unhappy.

So this virtuous circle soon turned to a vicious circle when Stayer's initial change exertions did not meet with success. "In short, the early 1980s were a disaster." After banging his head against the wall for two years, he came to a crucial insight:

"From now on," I announced to my management team, "you're all responsible for making your own decisions" I went from authoritarian control to authoritarian abdication. They were good soldiers and they did their best, but I had trained them to expect me to solve their problems. I had nurtured their inability by expecting them to be incapable. Now they met my expectations with an inability to make decisions unless they knew which decisions I wanted them to make. I wanted them to make the decisions I would have made. Deep down I was still in love with my own control.

In other words, a self-fulfilling prophecy dominated the organization and consisted of the original cycle of authoritarian expectation, the ensuing subordinate behavior, and the resulting success that reinforced the authoritarian expectation. Johnsonville Foods was so information-tight and isolated, that even pressure to change from Stayer himself was not effective.

It was only when Stayer began to understand the self-reinforcing effect at the bottom of the resistance that he shifted his entire change strategy. Later in the book, we shall see that Stayer learned from the early failures of his change efforts and eventually Johnsonville Foods went on to vast organizational changes.

The Self-Fulfilling Prophecy Is the Point of Transformation

Organizations or work groups under the thrall of a self-fulfilling prophecy simply are not open to information that counters the beliefs at the heart of the self-fulfilling prophecy. The circular, nonlinear structure of the beliefs establishes the context, or sets the range of possible actions in the system, and thereby acts as an attractor for the organization or work unit. This isolating, information-tight situation only gets worse as the self-fulfilling prophecy escalates nonlinearly and strengthens the original expectations. In an organization or work group, the circularity connecting the orginal belief, the consequent actions, and the resulting confirmation of the original belief forms a nonpermeable barrier around the organization's or work group's operation.

This stabilizing effect of the self-fulfilling prophecy seems to go against the example of Delta Airlines where the self-fulfilling prophecy provoked a clear departure from equilibrium in the growing proliferation of mistakes. The self-fulfilling prophecy, however, had formed a new equilibrium attractor that was based in making mistakes. This is what was so worrisome, no one seemed to know what changes to make to get the airline out of this mistake-prone equilibrium.

As we saw above, the structure of the self-fulfilling prophecy reveals a nonlinear interaction among beliefs, actions, and results. The inherent growth potential of its nonlinearity, however, is not apparent when the organization is in an equilibrium condition. In fact, just the opposite seems to be the case—the self-fulfilling prophecy keeps the organization at equilibrium and behaving in a linear fashion. In other words, even though the internal dynamic of the self-fulfilling prophecy is a nonlinear interaction, the self-fulfilling prophecy acts as the equilibrium attractor for the system by determining what is allowable and not allowable in terms of expectations, attitudes, and behaviors in the system. Paradoxically, the self-fulfilling prophecy is a nonlinear system that causes the organization to behave in a linear fashion.

This paradox is resolved by recognizing that the nonlinearity of the self-fulfilling prophecy refers to its *internal* structure or dynamics, while the linear and equilibrium effect are the result of the *external* function in the organization or work group system. The internal dynamic of the self-fulfilling prophecy is nonlinear because the actions that confirm the original belief increasingly amplify the belief. The function of the self-fulfilling prophecy is linear and maintains equilibrium because it is able to close the system to new information and new interactions with its environment. This equilibrium and linear maintainenance hide the nonlinearity that the self-fulfilling prophecy contains.

The most remarkable property of the *self-fulfilling prophecy as a nonlinear system is that it contains the seeds of its own transformation.* The key to change in organizations, therefore, lies in the growth potential inherent in the nonlinear nature of the self-fulfilling prophecy. This growth potential, however, is hidden and held in check at equilibrium conditions. In other words, the self-fulfilling prophecy contains its own seeds of transformation, but these seeds are not allowed to sprout at equilibrium conditions. Change, therefore consists of tapping into and unleashing the nonlinear growth potential inherent in the self-fulfilling prophecy. Paradoxically, the self-fulfilling prophecy is both the anchor of resistance in the system and the point of transformation.

The new model of change reveals that an equilibrium condition is not the final truth about organizations or work groups. They require far-from-equilibrium conditions to uncover the innate growth tendencies of nonlinear systems that are locked up in self-fulfilling prophecies.

Before we consider how far-from-equilibrium conditions can unleash the nonlinear growth potential hidden in organizations, we need to be able to recognize the many guises that a self-fulfilling prophecy can take. Identifying the self-fulfilling cycle that dominates a work group or organization, allows us to apply the appropriate far-from-equilibrium condition that will unleash its growth potential.

TYPES OF SELF-FULFILLING PROPHECIES

THE PYGMALION EFFECT

Ralph Stayer's original leadership style at Johnsonville Foods contained the self-fulfilling expectation that he was in control and his staff should follow only his direction. This expectation led to submissive behaviors from the staff, which reinforced his expectations. We can call this type of self-fulfilling prophecy in leadership the Pygmalion Effect, named after the Greek legend of Pygmalion, whose love for a statue he created of a beautiful woman resulted in the statue actually coming to life. The Pygmalion Effect describes a nonlinear, circular, and amplifying relation between a manager's expectations and employee performance.[6]

Social psychologist Robert Rosenthal investigated the Pygmalion Effect that occurs when a teacher's expectations strongly influence the quality of a student's performance.[7] In one famous study, teachers received false information about the grade-point averages and general intelligence levels of students in an incoming class. If the teacher was led to believe the student was at an "A" level, the student's performance on exams actually turned out better than if the teacher believed the student's level of achievement was low. Unbeknownst to the teacher, however, all the students were actually on the same academic level. Therefore, the effect on performance had to derive from the teacher's expectations alone; that is, it was a self-fulfilling prophecy. One explanation was that somehow the teacher unconsciously reinforced the "A" student more than the supposedly less gifted student.

Experiments have also shown that the Pygmalion Effect occurs in organizations and work groups. The expectations of supervisors, managers, and trainers and how they communicate have a difinite influence on employee performance. These expectations set up a self-fulfilling prophecy that is reinforced by successful outcomes. Trying to change the leadership style runs head-on into the Pygmalion Effect, which serves to maintain equilibrium and resist change.

The Pygmalion Effect as a self-fulfilling prophecy, however, is innately a nonlinear system and, therefore, contains the seed of its own transformation. Activating this seed requires an appropriate far-from-equilibrium condition that disrupts equilibrium and unleashes the growth potential in the organization. At Johnsonville Foods, the far-from-equilibrium condition that activated the seed of transformation was a change in leadership strategy. The CEO left important decisions entirely up to his staff, which allowed them to make mistakes. Eventually, this disrupted equilibrium to the extent that employees were allowed to decide whether or not Johnsonville would take on additional work.

THE JOSEPH EFFECT

As mentioned earlier, Delta Airlines saw a trend of mishaps that interfered with the operation of the company. Economist Edgar Peters relates how the eminent mathematician Benoit Mandelbrot named such a trend of occurrences the "Joseph Effect" after the biblical patriarch Joseph, who interpreted Pharoah's dream to mean there would be a trend of seven plentiful years, followed by a trend of seven years of famine.[8] In his analysis of data from capital markets such as stock and bond prices over long periods of time, Mandelbrot found trends, not simply random patterns. An example is the trend in which an increase in price continues to increase in the next period.

Peters metaphorically suggests that the existence of the Joseph Effect indicates the system has a kind of long-term memory that remembers and follows the trend. He speculates that this propensity is due to investors' biases, which are reinforced by the current direction of the stock price and what other investors are doing. The biases set up a mutually causal, self-fulfilling cycle so that as a price rises, other investors see a trend that confirms a positive bias for the stock, and they begin to buy as well. Again, this trend is the outcome of a self-fulfilling prophecy that amplifies an original tendency in a certain direction. The bias trend continues nonlinearly until new, random information about the company arrives to put an end to the upward escalation.

An example of how such a Joseph Effect can influence the dynamics of an organization is the case in which the VHS format of video recorders beat out the Beta format. According to economist W. Brian Arthur, when home VCRs first came out, both formats sold at about the same price.[9] Each format could realize increasing market returns by having its market share increased through video outlets stocking more tapes in one or the other of the formats. Then, whichever format was more well-stocked would lead consumers to prefer buying that format over the other. Here, a self-fulfilling cycle was created in which a small initial gain in market share improved the competitive advantage of one format, in this case VHS.

The truly interesting thing, as Arthur points out, is that both formats were introduced at about the same time, with the same initial market share. Luck or randomly increasing sales of VHS, however, tilted the competition toward VHS so it went on to win the battle, even though many claimed the Beta format was technically superior. We see here a small initial market lead, caused in large part by random fluctuations and amplified nonlinearly until it takes over and asserts its dominance.

This sort of self-fulfilling effect goes on all the time in organizations. For example, a hospital is considering purchasing a hospital-wide computer system and narrows their options to three vendors. A small random event may signal a bias toward one, such as the absence of senior managers at a showcase meeting. A trial run may amplify this random bias and then the hospital winds up buying the system.

Once the trend begins, though, it seems nearly impossible to change it. Consider how the information about the Beta format's superiority was unable to influence the system of buyers and vendors. The momentum of the self-fulfilling prophecy leads to resistance to change in the system. The challenge then, in a nonlinear self-fulfilling prophecy, is to generate a far-from-equilibrium condition that can interrupt the Joseph Effect.

THE PROCRUSTES EFFECT

Psychological experiments amply demonstrate that expectations about the roles people play in groups can become self-fulfilling prophecies. Persons playing those roles behave in ways that confirm the original expectations. We can call such a self-fulfilling prophecy the Procrustes Effect, after the pillager in Greek mythology who mutilated his victims to fit the length of his bed. The expectation about the role causes the person playing the role to behave in a manner that fits the role.

For example, in one psychological experiment, each subject was given a role of either *sender* or *target* and assigned to separate rooms that were connected electronically.[10] The senders received fabricated results of psychological tests that purportedly showed that the targets were hostile personalities. Consequently, the senders acted in a preemptively hostile manner to the targets. As a result, the targets, who did not know that the senders had received phony test results, responded antagonistically to the sender hostility. Of course, this simply confirmed the senders' erroneous original expectations and led to even more hostile behavior on the part of the senders.

What is even more astonishing is that when the original targets became senders to another group for which there were no phony hostile expectations, the original targets continued to be hostile, the new targets responded in kind, thus perpetuating the self-fulfilling prophecy in a new guilt-free generation.

This Procrustes Effect among expectations, roles, and behavior can be seen in the situation with the floor secretaries at "Parkside Hospital." Their resistance to change reflects a pattern of behavior in which survival depends on that pattern of behavior. Through years of learning how to survive and get the job done, the floor secretaries evolved a behavior that others in the hospital classified as abrupt, snappy, or nasty. The floor secretaries had become an isolated system that was information-tight, so that others' responses to them were only interpreted in terms of how they, internally, needed to survive. Therefore, the Procrustes Effect of their organizational roles was to resist changes being brought by the courtesy training program.

When the Procrustes Effect operates in an organization, a far-from-equilibrium condition can disrupt the self-fulfilling effect between organizational roles, expectations about the holders of those roles, and the ensuing behaviors. In other words, assumptions about roles need to be challenged in such a way that the self-fulfilling cycle is broken.

THE PLACEBO EFFECT

The Placebo Effect originally referred to how believing that a medicine is effective may lead to its being experienced as effective.[11] For example, someone with a headache can experience relief from the pain by taking medicine she or he believes is a painkiller, but is actually a pill made of an inert compound. That is why it is necessary to have double-blind studies in testing the effectiveness of pharmaceutical agents. *Double-blind* means that the persons taking the medicine are unaware of the potential effect of the substance being ingested, but the experimenters also are unaware of who is taking what medicine. The latter points out the power that expectations have in the self-fulfilling prophecies. They can be transmitted to the person taking the drug even by subtle nonverbal, unconscious ways. To insure validity in testing, all the relevant parties to the experiment must remain blind to the medicine's identity.

A classic case of the Placebo Effect is the patient with lymphoma who responded favorably to the cancer drug Krebiozen, popular in the mid-1950s.[12] Whenever the patient read in the paper that Krebiozen had been shown to be effective, his tumors shrank. When the same patient read that Krebiozen didn't work, however, the patient went downhill physically. This pattern of ups and downs continued for quite some time depending on the favorability of newspaper accounts. Unfortunately, the patient eventually succumbed when he read an article that Krebiozen was a fake and had no curative properties.

In organizations a similar Placebo Effect occurs in sociotechnical design, that is, the relation between persons and technology. Sociotechnical design is concerned with how people operating equipment or the technical system constrain the behavior of the technical system and, conversely, how the technical system constrains the behavior of the people. An example is the arrangement of computers and operators at "Wall

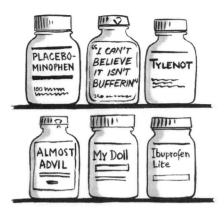

Street Stocks and Bonds," mentioned in Chapter 4. A self-fulfilling prophecy was at work in the relationship between the operators and the word processing computers and their arrangement. Expectations about the effectiveness of a certain arrangement of person and machine had a self-reinforcing effect on behaviors that were congruent with those expectations. The machine operators expected the machines to be a certain way, to work a certain way, to accomplish a certain amount, with a certain level of quality, in a certain process. When this expectation was acted on, the machines "complied" like a placebo working as an effective medicine; the operators accomplished what they expected (the patient got well) and attributed it to the efficacy of the machine (the patient attributes getting well to the medicine's remedial power). Variations in this self-reinforcing cycle are not tolerated—the system is information-tight, isolated, and shows a tendency to seek equilibrium, that is, it resists change.

Organizational change efforts having to do with a change in technology or the introduction of new technology will encounter the nonlinear, self-reinforcing Placebo Effect between person and machinery. This self-fulfilling prophecy requires a far-from-equilibrium condition to release the inherent self-organizing potential in the system.

THE IDENTITY EFFECT

The final type of self-fulfilling prophecy concerns the interaction of an organization's identity, its perception of the environment, and the ensuing strategic planning. For example, Gareth Morgan points out how a company will convene a strategy meeting to discuss the following key questions:[13]

Identity:

- What business are we in?

- Are we in the right business?

- What business should we be in?

Perception of Environment:

- What is our market?

Strategy:

- What is our strategy for penetrating our market?

The self-reinforcing effect can be seen in how the identity of the company ("What business are we in and should we be in?") is defined in reference to both the environment the company finds itself in ("What is our market?"), as well as the strategy the company has adopted until now ("What is our strategy for penetrating our market?"). It is a nonlinear, mutual influence because the market and the strategy are defined in reference to the identity of the company. In an important sense, the environment reflects the identity, and vice versa.

The sometimes disastrous, self-fulfilling effect of the Identity Effect can be seen in typewriter manufacturers at the time of the advent of word processors. If a firm identified itself as a manufacturer of typewriters, then it conceived its environment as the market that buys typewriters, and the strategy might be to undercut competition in that environment or have better quality or service in that market. Success in this arena would reinforce the self-fulfilling effect among the firm's identity, market perception, and strategy.

But this self-fulfilling prophecy acts as an isolated system that kept the firm from coming to a new sense of itself and its environment. Without the self-fulfilling prophecy to keep equilibrium and block new information, the firm might have made a transition to perceiving the market as purchasers of documents, not just typewritten materials. The more adamant the firm's identity as a typewriter maker, the more the firm disregarded the market signs that typewriters were going the way of the Edsel.

A similar point has been made by Ian Mitroff and Richard Mason in their study of the locked-in relation between strategy formulations and corporate assumptions.[14] Corporate assumptions have to do with the company's identity, its supposed strengths, weaknesses, capabilities, and so on. Strategy formulated on these assumptions only leads to actions that confirm these assumptions (when the company is successful). A problem occurs, however, when something goes wrong. The company's strategy is not successful, yet there seems nowhere to turn since this strategy is the only possibility considered in the context of their identity. Therefore, when self-fulfilling Identity Effects lead to resistance to change, far-from-equilibrium conditions are required to change the identity, strategy, and market assumptions inherent in the organization.[15]

Types of Nonlinear Self-Fulfilling Prophecies

• The Pygmalion Effect: Nonlinear interactions between leader expectations and employee behavior

• The Joseph Effect: Current behavior follows the trend of previous patterns no matter that random events caused these patterns

• The Procrustes Effect: Nonlinear interactions between job roles expectations about these roles, and the behavior of those occupying the role

• The Placebo Effect: Nonlinear interactions between expectations about technology and the use made of the technology

• The Identity Effect: How corporate identity, perception of the market, and strategy formulations are related in a nonlinear, self-fulfilling fashion

---

THE POINT OF RESISTANCE IS THE POINT OF TRANSFORMATION

The self-fulfilling prophecies discussed above share a common organizational effect: They reinforce a particular mode of attitude and action in such a way that attempts to change the organization run against this entrenched way of doing things. They are the places in the organizational system where change is resisted most strenuously. We have seen how, in the donkey model, this resistance becomes the identified enemy and a barrage of techniques are garnered to defeat it.

In the self-organization approach to system change, however, resistance as self-fulfilling prophecy is not a fortress to be stormed; it indicates the presence of an attractor—precisely the point where self-organizing transformation is unleashed. The key to this unleashing lies in the nonlinear growth potential hidden within the self-fulfilling prophecy.

As we saw in the case of the Benard liquid, when equilibrium dominates the system, the true nonlinear relationships inherent in the system are masked and appear linear. In the self-fulfilling nature of what is going on it is difficult to discern, and it is assumed the people in the work group or organization are simply resisting change. What is really happening though, is that self-fulfilling prophecies are maintaining equilibrium, and equilibrium conditions are making the system appear linear. The growth potential of nonlinearity just needs to be revealed, released, and activated.

Resistance then, and this is the crucial point, is what appears to be the case where the nonlinearity is present but hidden by equilibrium conditions. The nonlinearity is revealed under far-from-equilibrium conditions. Therefore, *whatever maintains a condition of resistance at equilibrium is the same process that leads to change at far-from-equilibrium conditions.* The nonlinearity will need to be unleashed so that its evolutionary potential can become manifest.

Whereas the self-fulfilling prophecy creates stability in a system under equilibrium conditions, *under far-from-equilibrium conditions, when the inherent nonlinearity of the self-fulfilling prophecy is revealed and released, the same effect can lead the system to transform itself.* In the former case the nonlinearity is masked, in the latter, far-from-equilibrium conditions unmask nonlinearity which brings out the evolutionary tendency.

This can be made clearer by an analogy shown in Figure 5-4. Imagine a golf ball resting in a deep bowl. If you move the ball up along the side of the bowl (move it away from equilibrium), it simply falls toward the bottom and eventually settles there again. In this stable system, the ball seeks to return to equilibrium. This equilibrium-seeking system of ball and bowl is like a self-fulfilling prophecy that operates to keep the beliefs and actions of the organization in line with prevalent norms. On the other hand, imagine a golf ball placed on the top of an inverted bowl with a curved bottom. A slight tap on bowl will send it careening down one side or the other. The ball will be propelled away from equilibrium. This represents a self-fulfilling prophecy under a far-from-equilibrium condition; a condition that amplifies departures from equilibrium in the organization.

In these two situations, the ball is switching from stable to unstable equilibrium. Therefore, the equilibrium, in and of itself, is not the problem. Instead, the problem lies in what attracts the system to the equilibrium state. The self-fulfilling prophecy is just this mechanism that can attract the system to the equilibrium condition. That is why a far-from-equilibrium condition must interrupt the self-fulfilling prophecy: to release the energy locked inside toward transforming the system.

In human systems, because they are nonlinear, self-fulfilling cycles are always present. The issue is whether we use them to create unchanging, information-tight situations or whether we release its tendency toward growth. This hinges on whether the system is at equilibrium or far from equilibrium. The solution to resistance, therefore, is not to add more pressure for change (a linear remedy), but to create the conditions that will release for self-organization the tremendous power locked up in the resistance.

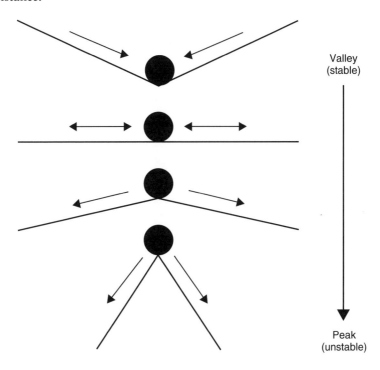

Valley
(stable)

Peak
(unstable)

Figure 5-4. From Equilibrium to Far-From-Equilibrium

The challenge is to find the right far-from-equilibrium conditions to match the specific nonlinearity involved in the self-fulfilling prophecies. This entails recognizing the nonlinear two-way causality that operates in the self-fulfilling prophecy and removing the insularity that surrounds it. The following chapters suggest how to generate far-from-equilibrium conditions in organizations and work groups in order to release this tendency toward change and development. Self-fulfilling effects are not going to go away; they are essential in the mutually interactive reality of human systems. We must learn to harness the self-fulfilling effect for change instead of resistance.

GENERATING FAR-FROM-EQUILIBRIUM
CONDITIONS

When you come to an impasse, change;
If you change, you can get through.
—I CHING (CHENG YI COMMENTARY)

Businesses, hospitals, government bureaucracies, charitable foundations, community agencies, and utilities are undergoing organizational transformations that we could not even imagine twenty years ago. Some of these changes are truly radical, literally going to the root of what a viable organization is all about. This is why the model of self-organization is so attractive—it demonstrates radical transformation.

Let's keep in mind how self-organization occurs. It requires a nonlinear system and far-from-equilibrium conditions. Understanding this entails an entirely new formulation of deeply rooted system change, as well as a reconsideration of how this radical transformation occurs. Consequently, the method of change becomes as radical as the outcome of the change process.

It's no different for facilitating organizational transformation. If you want deeply rooted change, you need to apply deeply rooted methods. Unlike traditional methods, which are steeped in a linear and equilibrium model, the new methods must be attuned to nonlinearity and be able to generate far-from-equilibrium conditions. In other words, we must upset the apple-cart, uproot the roots, and rock the boat.

It is crucial to recognize, however, that this doesn't involve an increase in managerial pressure, top-down interference, or huge investments of effort. Those are just continuations of the old way, in which change is the result of external pressure on a system. The new way must be deep, but it can also be subtle in the way it facilitates the conditions whereby self-organization occurs as a spontaneous and internally driven process. Self-organization simply does not take place as the result of hierarchical imposition.

In the last chapter we explored how organizations can be understood as nonlinear systems whose inherent growth potential is held in check by equilibrium-seeking processes. Moreover, from Chapter 3 we learned what far-from-equilibrium conditions look like in a simple physical system and how they unleash the evolutionary potential of a nonlinear system. Now, we need to make the transition from simple physical systems to the realm of our businesses and institutions.

ORGANIZATIONAL TRANSFORMATION AT JOHNSONVILLE FOODS

As a start in this direction, let's take another look at Johnsonville Foods, which underwent a successful and deeply rooted organizational transformation. What happened at Johnsonville Foods can give us clues about what is involved in radical organizational change.

In the last chapter we left Ralph Stayer, the CEO of Johnsonville Foods, in the middle of a dilemma: his efforts to change the company were floundering. Yet all the ingredients for change seemed to be in place. Certainly, there was a new corporate vision as well as commitment from top management. After all, it was Stayer's vision—he was top management fervently pushing for change: "I spent two years pursuing another mirage as well—detailed strategic and tactical plans that could realize my goal...We tried to plan organizational structure two to three years before it would be needed—my business training told me this was the way to proceed." Yet no one was buying into the new philosophy of shared responsibility for making decisions. Stayer was indeed baffled.

What Stayer came to realize was how his own leadership expectations were hindering his change intentions: "I had created the management style that kept people from assuming responsibility." Stayer was up against the powerful equilibrium-maintaining force of the self-fulfilling prophecy derived from his leadership expectations and reinforced by the past success of the company. His past success had become his present problem. It was this self-fulfilling structure that blocked the efforts to change Johnsonville Foods.

With Stayer's realization came a shift in focus: "The goal was not so much a state of shared responsibility as an environment where people insist on being responsible." This called for a shift in context, a shift in what attracted the expectations and actions in the company. But this, in turn, meant Stayer had to transform the very way he implemented change. His problem was that he was imposing his desire for empowerment the same way he had previously imposed his management prerogatives; he would try to overpower any resistance to the imposition.

Stayer recognized the nature of the impasse, but only after hitting his head against the wall for two years. "After two years of stewing, it began to dawn on me that my first reactions to most situations were dead wrong. After all, my organizational instincts had brought me to Point A to begin with. Pursuing those instincts now would only bring us back to Point A." As the saying goes: insanity is expecting different results for doing the same thing over and over again!

Stayer redirected his change efforts and succeeded in unleashing the potential for change inherent in the corporation. The result was that Johnsonville Foods evolved into one of the most successful examples of participatory and team environments in the United States. Here are some of the benchmarks of this unleashing of change at Johnsonville:

- Teams of line workers who make the products, rather than quality control inspectors, became responsible for quality control. The spontaneous reorganization of quality control was not the result of the imposition of a formal Total Quality Management program. In fact, it occurred way before TQM had become a buzzword. The quality control department became a technical support function.

- Line workers became directly connected to both suppliers and retail stores. Customer letters were forwarded not to customer service representatives or even to managers but directly to the work teams making the sausages. The work teams themselves then responded to complaints.

- Many previous managerial decisions shifted to the line worker teams such as schedules, performance standards, assignments, budgets, quality measures, and even capital improvements. The managers, renamed *coordinators* or *coaches,* acted more as facilitators and teachers than as authoritarian leaders. Workers renamed themselves *members*. As Stayer says, those managers who needed the old style of authority left the company.

- Line worker teams took on several crucial human resource responsibilities: the selection and training of new workers; performance evaluation of peers, including determination of compensation; and even the firing of individuals who didn't perform to the work teams' standards. The personnel department became a learning and personal development team.

- The design of a new compensation system that consisted of two major elements:

  1. Pay for responsibility: learning new duties and skills leads to a pay increase;

  2. Company performance share: a fixed percentage of pre-tax profits to be divided every six months and shared according to the work team's performance appraisal.

We see in these changes at Johnsonville Foods many elements of self-organization: coordination of the parts of a system in new, more coherent patterns; self-generated, rather than hierarchically-imposed, functioning; use of the system's own resources to find new ways of doing things; and new connections of systems to their environments. Indeed, the donkey model of change and resistance cannot even begin to encompass the far-reaching changes that occurred in nearly every system and structure at Johnsonville. Only a model of self-organization, with its dynamics of spontaneous systemic restructuring can encompass the type of radical organizational transformation that occurred at Johnsonville.

Stayer managed to unleash the evolutionary urge toward self-organization. According to the new model of system change, this is a matter of placing a nonlinear system under the appropriate far-from-equilibrium conditions. Therefore, we are now at the stage where we can explore how our businesses and institutions can generate far-from-equilibrium conditions.

Let's turn back to the main features of far-from-equilibrium conditions described in Chapter 3. Far-from-equilibrium conditions:

- activate nonlinearity to prompt system change

- interrupt equilibrium-seeking processes

- amplify departures from equilibrium
- need to match the system's nonlinearity
- require firm but permeable system boundaries
- challenge a system to restructure its mode of organization
- contain an element of unpredictability

We need to translate and incorporate these seven features into their organizational counterparts. A far-from-equilibrium condition, by definition, is an interference with those factors that are maintaining equilibrium in a system. Therefore, we can start the process of translation by taking a closer look at the dynamics of equilibrium-seeking in work organizations. If we know exactly what's involved with equilibrium-seeking, then we will be in better position to understand what's involved with moving a system out of equilibrium.

ORGANIZATIONS AT EQUILIBRIUM ARE LOW IN INFORMATION

First of all, in the last chapter, we examined how the self-fulfilling prophecy is the primary culprit for an equilibrium-seeking mechanism because it blocks information. The self-fulfilling prophecy has this power because it is self-confirming, it does not require external confirmation. Therefore, it is only open to information that flows within its insular structure, information that connects beliefs, behaviors, and results in a self-fulfilling manner. At the same time, new information that accompanies any attempt at organizational change is not allowed to enter the system.

The insular nature of the self-fulfilling prophecy characterizes its role as an attractor of the system. As such, it demarcates the acceptable behavior of the system and continually returns the system to its original equilibrium when a change temporarily disturbs the system out of equilibrium. When undergoing transformation a system passes out of one attractor regime and into another. This passage is brought about by a far-from-equilibrium condition that unleashes the evolutionary thrust of the system.

Since in an organization, one aspect of equilibrium-seeking is the refusal to admit new information into the system, an important aspect of a far-from-equilibrium condition is to allow new information into the system. What, however, is meant by "information" and how can it be allowed into a system?

ORGANIZATIONAL INFORMATION IS NOT MERE DATA

In Chapter 3 we saw how heat exchange between an environment and a system can lead to far-from-equilibrium conditions that facilitate self-organization. In organizations and work groups, the commodity of exchange is information. We need to distinguish information from mere data, however, since in these days of information-processing, the term information is often used interchangeably with the term *data*.

Data refers to facts or figures, as in a spread-sheet. *Information, however, refers to the knowledge that is available to a system of its own functioning, of the arrangement of its parts, where each element is and what it is doing.* Whereas data is a set of facts, information in a social system goes beyond facts about the system to the relationship between the facts, or among the people in the system who know the facts. For example, if the husband in a family says "I am depressed," it is data, since it is a report about the person himself rather than in relation to another. But if the husband says, "I am depressed when my wife looks at me with an angry face," this is information because it is about the relationship between the members of the social system.[1] As information, the hus-

band's remarks are about the pattern of relationship—in other words the organization of the family system.

In a work setting, data might consist of someone in a work group saying "I am tired," "It was a late shipment," or "He is a terrible boss." These statements express facts about how someone felt or perceived something or someone, and therefore, express data. But, information would be about a *relationship* in the group. For example, the same person might say "I am tired because our great and wonderful leader, Tom, had to get that report to the CEO, and he recommended strongly I stay with him and help him finish it." Here is more than just a simple statement of what someone felt; here is information that says something about the perception of the relationship between the subordinate and the boss. The social system of the work place is, after all, nothing more than the complex interaction of everyone in the work place, and information is the knowledge available to the system about the patterns of organization in this complex interaction.

Consider the following scenario offered by Jeremy Campbell to illustrate the concept of information.[2] Imagine a typical library where books are arranged according to the Dewey decimal system. If you know the call letters, it is easy to find a book on corporate finance. The orderly way the books in the library are labeled and put on the shelves is analogous to a system in a high state of organization. In such a system *information* is high since the knowledge of how the system is ordered and how the parts relate to one another is available (where a book is located and how to retrieve it). In this state of high information and structured order, the librarians must expend a lot of time and effort to organize the books. Therefore, it is not a system in rest or equilibrium because of the need to expend energy continually to maintain the order.

Then imagine the same library after a long period of neglect, in which books were not replaced according to their call letters, but were randomly placed on the closest shelf. Very little effort was spent to maintain the organization, and as a result, the order dissolved. This random library is in a state of rest or equilibrium because it is the state the system tended towards when no effort was expended to keep it organized. In this equilibrium state, the information is low, because it is next to impossible to retrieve a book on corporate finance among the thousands of disorganized books. In other words, since the system does not have the knowledge of itself available to itself, it is in a state of low information.

Information, then, is knowledge available to the system concerning how it is organized, how the parts of the system relate to one another, how it is structured or patterned, and how things are exchanged across the system. It can be said information is about the organization of the system.

We already discussed how self-fulfilling prophecies are information-tight, that is, the circular, mutually causal relationship between expectations or beliefs, actions, and the resulting confirmation create an isolated system that keeps out new information. This was seen in Chapter 5 in the example of the typewriter companies that were not open to new information about their market or the unexpected competition from word processors. This information, had it been allowed to enter the company's system, would have made a difference. It would have challenged the existing identity of the company as merely a manufacturer of typewriters.

Resistance to change as the effect of a self-fulfilling prophecy, therefore, manifests a tendency to diminish information. But, resistance, as we have been pointing out, is not really resistance, it is simply a description of a system under the influence of an equilibrium attractor. This means that resistance and equilibrium conditions are characterized by low information. That is, the system in question does not have access to knowledge about how it is organized, about patterns of relationships among the parts of the system.

ORGANIZATIONAL EQUILIBRIUM DOES NOT GENERATE NEW INFORMATION

Consider this low information exchange between a manager and subordinate as the boss walks around the work site:

> Boss: Hi, how's it going?
> Employee: Fine.
> Boss: What's happening?
> Employee: Nothing new really.
> Boss: Well, it's good to hear that everything's okay.

This conversation does not introduce any new information into the system, except perhaps the news that nothing much is new. This kind of transaction is fairly typical and represents a system at equilibrium. In fact, communication theorists point out that many organizational mechanisms filter and even stop the flow of real information in an organization, for example the mum effect in which people are reluctant to spread correct, but possibly bad, news upward. Another example is the status effect, whereby people higher in the hierarchy are not as willing to talk to those below.

Here is another example of a meeting where information is kept low and equilibrium is maintained:

> Staff Member (Bill): I need to bring up an issue about the new benefits policy.
> Boss (Jim): You don't have to say anything. I know all about it.
> Staff Member: But Jim, many of the employees are saying...
> Boss: Believe me! There's nothing you can say. I know what's going on.
> Staff Member: Jim, we really have to look . . .
> Boss: Listen, I'll take care of it!

In this dialogue, again, not much information is transmitted. Instead, the boss squelches information by anticipating what will be said, and uses his prerogative, and probably repetitive, management style to prevent a free flow of information, especially if it departs from his perspective.

We see that the norms or patterns of behavior keeps information low in this work group, which is equivalent to keeping the group in equilibrium. Equilibrium in a social system, therefore, is the same as a condition of low information in the social system.

FAR-FROM-EQUILIBRIUM CONDITIONS GENERATE INFORMATION

In our contemporary businesses, data streams in from all sides as a result of the high-tech revolution. But, this increase in data does not necessarily lead to transformation; in fact, it often leads to analysis paralysis—no one is quite sure what to do with all the data. Data, therefore, does not always become information.

Far-from-equilibrium conditions, however, increase the information in an organization or work group. For example, compare a system at equilibrium, with the same system after self-organization has taken place, for example, the Benard system before and after heating. At equilibrium the parts of the system do not differ much from each other. After self-organization, however, the liquid is so highly organized and structured that one part of the system is very different than the other parts of the system. We can say the system at equilibrium and sameness has lower information than the self-organized system, because of the different ways that the parts relate in each phase of the system.

This makes information a crucial concept in a model of change based on self-organization. Self-organization reorganizes a system's patterns of relationships among its parts, which changes the information in the system. Therefore, to bring about change in a social system, according to the model of self-organization, would increase the information in the system. Since equilibrium (and low information) is maintained by self-fulfilling prophecies, then a far-from-equilibrium condition is the factor that interrupts the self-fulfilling prophecy and, consequently, breaks down the information barrier that the self-fulfilling prophecy established.

Breaking down the barrier and allowing information in a far-from-equilibrium condition increases the knowledge available to a system about its own functioning. Any means that can increase this available knowledge can also provoke a far-from-equilibrium condition. In fact, whatever leads to radical organizational transformation with the kind of deeply rooted change associated with self-organization probably has this far-from-equilibrium tendency to generate information even if that is not the overt purpose of the intervention.

GENERATING FAR-FROM-EQUILIBRIUM CONDITIONS IN ORGANIZATIONS

WORKING WITH ORGANIZATIONAL BOUNDARIES

Chapter 3 demonstrated that self-organization requires a strongly bounded arena to contain nonlinear transformations. Similarly, organizational transformation that follows the model of self-organization requires that the arenas demarcated for change be characterized by firm boundaries. Boundaries, in this sense, refer to the structural boundaries between an organization and its environment, as well as the internal boundaries between functions inside the organization. Boundaries also refer to the psychological boundaries constituted by patterns of power, authority, decision-making, and so on. If the boundaries in an organization are too weak, the system will not be able to withstand the increase of information that the far-from-equilibrium conditions generate.

That is why an important step in the generation of far-from-equilibrium conditions consists of firming up the boundaries between work groups, organizations, and their environments. In fact, this is a necessary first step before other far-from-equilibrium methods can be initiated. Working with organizational boundaries is covered in more detail in Chapter 7.

CONNECTING SYSTEMS TO ENVIRONMENTS

Firming boundaries is only half the boundary work self-organization requires. The boundaries must also be permeable enough to allow vital exchange with the system's environments. Therefore, a crucial phase of facilitating far-from-equilibrium conditions includes connecting work groups and organizations with their environments.

The environments of work groups include other work groups within the organization, as well as suppliers of raw materials, customers, and so on. The environments of organizations include customers, suppliers, governmental agencies, the community, and trade associations; therefore, the role of the change agent is not only to focus on the internal dynamics of the organization or work group, but also to be a bridge between the internal system and the system's environments. Connecting systems to environments is covered in detail in Chapter 7.

DIFFERENCE QUESTIONING

It is important to uncover and highlight differences in attitudes, perceptions, expectations, beliefs, or points of view in a work group. They are the cornerstones of the self-fulfilling prophecies that foster resistance to change in the organization. So, questioning differences is a way of churning up the underlying foundation of self-fulfilling prophecies.

Difference questioning is exactly opposite to the usual practice of consensus-seeking. Achieving consensus, which is often done prematurely, can be a subtle form of group conformity. When members of a group question differences, however, they, themselves, generate the new information. The facilitator's role is to keep the focus on differences, not premature agreement. Difference questioning is covered in Chapter 8.

PURPOSE CONTRASTING

Every organization has the purpose to create a product or provide a service. However, the purpose of work groups inside an organization is to help the organization achieve its goal. Often, however, an organization or work group is not effective in achieving its purpose. For example, in an entrenched bureaucratic institution, maintaining the bureaucratic hierarchy and enforcing all the consequent rules, procedures and regulations can supersede the original purpose of the organization.

Information can be generated by contrasting the original purpose of a work group or organization with the purpose of its current functioning. The group members themselves do this. No one else tells them what their purpose should be, not their boss nor a TQM or reengineering specialist. Telling workers what their purpose should be is just more new wine put into old wine skins, just more imposition and subsequent opposition. Chapter 8 goes into more detail about purpose contrasting.

FAR-FROM-EQUILIBRIUM CHALLENGES

Since self-fulfilling prophecies act as barriers to new information, the self-fulfilling cycles are themselves identified and challenged. Information, therefore, is generated directly on these circular, equilibrium-maintaining activities. Challenges such as these directly confront the systemic dimension of the self-fulfilling effects, that is, how a self-fulfilling prophecy contaminates creativity and innovation in the system.

Because of the nonlinear nature of the self-fulfilling prophecies, a far-from-equilibrium challenge need not be a huge endeavor. Often, small key elements of the self-fulfilling cycle can be identified and challenged, leading to an unexpected large effect. Far-from-equilibrium challenges are discussed in detail in Chapter 9.

CHALLENGING ASSUMPTIONS CREATIVELY

Techniques and exercises in creative thinking can also reveal the assumptions underlying the self-fulfilling prophecies in an organization. Revealing and challenging them brings new information into the group. Again, it is the persons involved in the change who evoke this new information, not representatives of hierarchical control.

Creativity exercises are powerful tools for freeing thinking from the stagnation of an organization or work group functioning at equilibrium. Not only can they help in problem-solving or decision-making, but they can also generate new information about the system that can foster self-organizing transformation. Challenging assumptions is discussed further in Chapter 9.

NONVERBAL REPRESENTATIONS OF THE SYSTEM

Not all information is available in verbal form; that is, not all information comes in the form of an idea or on the level of conscious thought. Some information is encoded nonverbally in the structures, relationships, and practices in organizations and work groups. Uncovering nonverbal information requires nonverbal methods.

For example, one nonverbal technique is a group "sculpture," in which members physically arrange themselves in relation to one another as a representation of the group's patterns of relationships. Such a nonverbal approach emphasizes that information is also embodied in the emotional and physical terrain of a work group or organization. Chapters 9 and 10 cover nonverbal approaches in detail.

TAKING ADVANTAGE OF CHANCE AND SERENDIPITY

An element of unpredictability characterizes self-organization. A system can use random departures from equilibrium to create and facilitate a new structure. Therefore, information in organizations can reside in organizational "noise" or random, mostly neglected, departures from an organization's equilibrium. Far-from-equilibrium methods enable the organization or work group to notice, use, and amplify this noise, and thereby turn it into new information.

The noise that will prove useful, and how this noise is used, however, are largely a matter of chance. Successful organizational transformation is frequently the serendipitous transformation of noise into useful information. Chapter 10 discusses this in detail.

Methods to Generate Far-from-Equilibrium Conditions and Self-Organization

• Working with organizational boundaries

• Connecting systems to environments

• Difference questioning

• Purpose contrasting

• Far-from-equilibrium challenges

• Challenging assumptions creatively

• Nonverbal representations of the system

• Taking advantage of chance and serendipity

• Using absurdity

USING ABSURDITY

In an organization or work group at equilibrium conditions, everything proceeds as it always has. Usually a far-from-equilibrium condition is needed to jar the system out of its routine. Some interventions use elements of absurdity to bring about the far-from-equilibrium conditions to achieve this.

To paraphrase the famous saying from Pascal: nonlinearity has reasons that reason knows nothing of. To change a nonlinear system requires a new kind of nonlinear rationality, perhaps appearing absurd from the perspective of the stodgy equilibrium-maintaining atmosphere in the system. Chapter 10 goes over this new kind of nonlinear rationality.

WORKING WITH BOUNDARIES

Unlimited possibilities are not suited to man;
if they existed, his life would dissolve in the boundless.
To become strong, a man's life needs...limitations...
—I CHING (COMMENTARY BY RICHARD WILHELM)

More and more, people are using the term *chaos* to describe their experience of working in corporations undergoing unprecedented change. We also hear a lot about the need to turn organizations into *open systems*, in which new types of contact between an organization and its environments supplant traditionally defined boundaries. At the same time, there has been a dismantling of internal boundaries between manager and employee, between headquarters and field operations, and between one department and another.

Amidst all this dismantling of boundaries, there seems to be a rising belief that to facilitate deeply rooted organizational change is merely a matter of introducing chaos anywhere and everywhere in an organization. The emphasis is shifting to the belief that if we create enough disorganization, a better mode of operating will emerge from the ensuing anarchy. The popularization of *chaos theory* only adds fuel to this disruption in the work place. Perhaps some of the readers of this book even think that is where we are going. After all, the term *far-from-equilibrium* appears to have this connotation of disruption and agitation.

Challenging traditional boundaries and structures is, indeed, an important step in facilitating organizational transformation. However, it needs to be emphasized that self-organization is always re-organization. This means that self-organization involves transformation by challenging currently existing patterns and structures. It is not a process that takes

[handwritten note in left margin:] not necessarily t ?

place in the midst of total anarchy. Because self-organization represents an optimization of pattern plus variety,[1] new structures will emerge in the place of old structures and new connections to the environment will emerge in the place of old connections.

Larry Hirschhorn and Tom Gilmore have called attention to the attendant increase of anxiety and confusion in today's *boundaryless organization*.[2] Facile talk about introducing chaos or traversing boundaries simply ignores the extremely critical, but paradoxical, role that boundaries play in the process of self-organization.

On the one hand, self-organization only occurs within a firmly bounded arena. This firm boundary limits and channels the nonlinear processes that occur in the system. For example, in the transformation of the Benard liquid, self-organizing convection cells can emerge only in a vessel that keeps the liquid from leaking out or evaporating. The vessel is a firm boundary that contains the process of self-organization.

On the other hand, self-organization requires that this firm boundary also be permeable so that exchange can occur between the system and its environment. In fact, this exchange aids in generating a far-from-equilibrium condition. So, the boundary must be both firm and permeable.

In the new model of organizational change, the dual process of firming as well as traversing organizational boundaries must accompany the generation of far-from-equilibrium conditions. This work with boundaries is so important we must consider it before we describe the various other methods for generating far-from-equilibrium conditions. Let's take a look at an example of organizational change where boundary issues were paramount.

AN OPEN SYSTEM THAT WAS TOO OPEN

Fort Chesterton's "Community Emergency Response Center" ("CERC") is the town's administrative office overseeing emergency medical services that include three ambulances, a mobile intensive care unit, professional staff, and a large coterie of volunteers. "CERC" is run by a director, an administrator in charge of finances, and an administrator who supervises both program development for volunteers as well as fund-raising. As in many community agencies, a Board of Trustees from the community superintends the operation. In the case of "CERC," the chairman of the board often interferes with its operations. The finance administrator experienced the intrusion most intensely, since the chairman is the president of a local bank.

"CERC"'s director decided to bring in an external consultant in order to begin a process of becoming a more effective agency. At the first meeting, the administrators discussed what they thought were the main problems with the agency. The director talked about the operation of the agency and her view of it as an "open space." The finance person, however, expressed how overwhelmed she felt, in part because of the intrusion from the chairman into this *open space*, and also because she didn't feel adequately supported to do her job.

As the consultant observed the operation of "CERC," she noticed how the open space concept breached boundaries in several facets of the organization. The administrative offices were in an open area where volunteers could come and use the copy machine whenever they wanted—anyone, for that matter, could come and go whenever they liked. The director not only didn't screen any of the calls, she would talk to anyone who happened to come by. In addition, no one could tell the male custodian what to do or even challenge him about such matters as when the building was to be closed up for the night.

At the second meeting, the consultant summarized issues from the first meeting and asked if anything happened in the interim. While the finance person expressed more frustration, the director remarked on the physical discomfort she was experiencing due to her bad back, suggesting several times that she might not last the whole session. At the next two meetings, a similar pattern was repeated, but whenever the consultant brought remarks back to the concept of the open space management style, the director switched the focus back to the intrusion of the chairman and what they should do. At the end of the fourth meeting, the director spent a few minutes talking to the consultant by herself, thanking her for working with the group, and stating that they could now continue without her. The director mentioned that they would move the copy machine, and that she was glad that issues had come out into the open.

As the consultant reviewed the intervention, she recognized that the very way the consultation was initiated included yet another breach of a boundary, this time, an important psychological boundary. That is, even though the consultant wanted to begin the intervention by interviewing each person separately, the director insisted that issues be raised by the group as a whole rather than through private interviews. Moreover, the consultant also realized that the intervention lacked a contract that would have established a clear and firm boundary within which the group's functioning could be safely challenged. The lack of a clear and firm boundary in the organizational change intervention itself reflected the other boundary transgressions that were affecting "CERC."

THE ROLE OF BOUNDARIES IN
ORGANIZATIONAL CHANGE

In this day of tumultuous change, organizations will try anything that promises to help them become more responsive: flattening management pyramids, setting up cross-functional, self-managed work groups, changing the manager's role to that of a coach, and so on. The old rules, the old norms, the old guiding principles, the old *boundaries* no longer hold sway.

In this context, it may appear at first sight that breaching boundaries at "CERC" was a progressive, constructive way to manage the agency. This lack of boundaries might seem to represent a system in close, vital contact with its environments; seemingly what we've been prescribing by offering a model of change based on self-organization.

Even the influence of so-called *open systems* theory in management studies has given the impression that effective organizations are essentially adaptive mechanisms whose open receptivity to every environmental change should automatically and immediately lead to a corresponding shift in the organization itself. This *open systems* approach implies that the more open the organization is to its environment, the more effective it is supposed to be. Therefore, it would seem that a system continually needs to breach those boundaries that isolate it from the environment.

Let's refer back to Hirschhorn's and Gilmore's study of the psychological effect of the *boundaryless* organization that has removed traditional barriers between hierarchical levels, across functional areas, and between the organization and its various environments. Hirschhorn and Gilmore emphasize that the excision of traditional boundaries only creates the need for a new set of boundaries that are more psychological than organizational. Traditional boundaries provide a precise set of guidelines to help maintain clarity and cut down on ambiguity. Employees know what to do, whom to report to, what is expected of them, and so on. Without these traditional boundaries anxiety, conflict, and friction increase, sometimes to the point of paralysis.

In the *boundaryless* organization, then, it is necessary to establish new boundaries to replace the old, dismantled ones. Hirschhorn and Gilmore give the example of boundaries around the issue of *authority*. Everyone in the organization demands a protocol for decision-making, as well as for accountability, established in the context of relationships of authority (though not necessarily authoritarian relationships). When the relationships of authority between a manager and subordinate are clear and strong, the manager sets the boundary and context for the subordinate's work. Establishing subtle, but strong, psychological boundaries that clarify who has final responsibility for decisions enables subordinates to then negotiate changes within these boundaries (a process not found in an authoritarian relationship). A successful authority boundary can contain potentially destructive conflict.

The transition from authoritarian to authority boundaries can be a rough journey. As the old boundary is being transformed, at certain stages, the old boundary is very weak, yet the new boundary is not firmly established. According to Hirshhorn and Gilmore, new boundaries need to be demarcated in the following four organizational areas:

- Authority: Who is in charge of what?

- Task: Who does what?

- Political: What's in it for us?

- Identity: Who is—and isn't—us?

Boundary Problems at "National Electro-Comm"

Boundary problems were at the heart of the difficult situation at "National Electro-Comm," described in Chapter 3. The issue was with the lack of an authority boundary on the part of the vice president of R&D, who refused to take on the appropriate mantle of leadership. He was failing both to direct what was going on and to say forthrightly what needed to be accomplished. He felt that exercising his authority would hurt his subordinates. This belief was central to a self-fulfilling prophecy at work in the situation: the leader's lack of authority boundaries led to fragile behavior on the part of his subordinates, which, in turn, confirmed the need for the vice president to take on a caretaking role.

One effect of the lack of clear boundaries was the isolation of individuals within the division, as well as the isolation of the division from the rest of the organization. At first sight, it seems that the lack of firm boundaries allows for less isolation. But, and this is a crucial point, the lack of clear and firm boundaries damages a system's integrity to the point that the parts of the system defensively reinforce isolation. It's as if *isolation becomes a substitute for the lack of firm boundaries*, at least to the extent that isolation prevents the system and its part from leaking into the environment.

Shoring up and firming the leadership boundaries was essential to the success of the program. The firming of the boundary created the safe container where the rest of the division could go about their work more effectively.

Establishing firm boundaries around these issues provides the foundation for a healthy organization.

Let's take a look at an organizational change intervention at a medical school where the issue of boundaries was a crucial element in the change process.

ESTABLISHING FIRM BOUNDARIES AT A MEDICAL SCHOOL

A medical school dean and his faculty were developing a new strategic planning process.[3] As a preliminary step, they gathered information by interviewing key faculty and fed it back to a group of about twenty-five chairpersons and researchers. At first, the consultants designing the project wanted to conduct the feedback sessions in small groups, but the faculty absolutely refused, preferring, instead, to talk in plenary.

The consultants later realized that splitting the faculty up would have been a mistake for it would have damaged the already weak boundaries that currently existed in the organization. A medical school is already an under-bounded system because of the individualistic spirit of physicians. In addition, the report was going to be tough on the school and some faculty members would feel attacked. Therefore, the group needed to experience the boundary around the whole system before they could work safely in small groups and absorb the implications of the report. Splitting up would only have created feelings of fragmentation. Therefore, during this kind of change process, a change agent needs to ask: where is the boundary now and where should it be?

SYSTEMS, BOUNDARIES, AND ENVIRONMENTS

In order to better understand the critical need to work with boundaries during the process of organizational transformation, we need to explore in further depth the concepts of system, environment, and boundaries. First, consider a contained liquid. Why does this liquid seem more like a system than a bunch of stones strewn on the ground? In a system there is more connection between the parts. Certainly, there is some relationship among rocks strewn along the ground, as well as between people on a line at the supermarket. It is also clear, though, that the degree of connection is much greater among the members of a family than it is among strangers in the supermarket line. For the purposes of this book, a system will be defined as an assemblage of parts where the degree of relationship among the parts is unmistakable and strongly contrasted with a random assemblage of parts.

In a system, as opposed to a mere ensemble of individuals, the parts have an influence on each other. In the case of a contained liquid, the different regions of liquid are able to influence other regions through chemical interactions stimulated by a flow of currents or waves. This type of mutual influence is a property of nonlinearity discussed in Chapter 2. Nonlinear systems are those in which there is an unmistakable influence of the parts on one another. Work units and business organizations are clearly nonlinear systems.

Let's be more specific and look at the ways in which the Benard liquid is a *system*. The container acts as a boundary that limits the liquid it contains. Liquids, of course, need such containers as boundaries to keep them from spreading out and losing their identity as a discrete entity. This sense of being a discrete entity is a hallmark of a system. The Benard liquid has this identity, but a group of stones strewn on the ground does not, for there is no way for us to distinguish these stones *here* as significantly different from those stones over *there*.

The boundary of a system creates the identity of the system and defines it in contrast to its environment (see Figure 7-1). The system is internal to the boundary and the environment is external. This distinction of internal from external, of system from environment, characterizes a system.

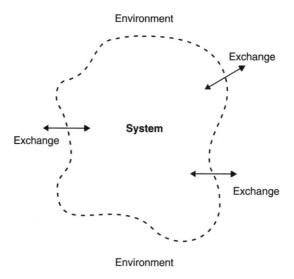

Figure 7-1. Exchange Between System and Environment

In the Benard system, the boundary between system and environment was breached when the heat was turned on. It is crucial to note, however, that the boundary didn't disappear; it simply was traversed to effectuate an exchange with the environment. In self-organization, boundaries have to be nonpermeable enough to contain the system, yet permeable enough to allow an exchange with the environment.

SELF-ORGANIZATION REQUIRES A BOUNDED SYSTEM

It is a truism to say organizations and work groups are systems. Certainly, this is not a controversial point.[4] Various schools understand organizations as systems. These perspectives all emphasize the ways that organizations function, which indicates that the way organizations function can't be understood simply as the behavior of parts in a nonsystemic ensemble.

It is crucial to recognize that only if a system is intact, unique, and whole is it able to self-organize. For example, the differences in internal temperature and density that determines the far-from-equilibrium conditions in the Benard system can only challenge it to reorganize if the liquid is an intact system to begin with. If the system's boundaries are violated so that it is no longer intact, then the Bernard liquid is no longer a system that can self-organize. For instance, if the heat melts a hole in the container, the liquid would leak out at a rate that would increase as the temperature gets hotter. Then, there would no longer be a Benard system. Accordingly, the container as boundary must be strong and firm enough to keep the system intact.

The *open systems* approach emphasizes a system's ability to be affected by the environment. In self-organized systems, the emphasis is on an internal process within firmly demarcated boundaries. In this sense, self-organization requires a *closed system*, and, at the same time, the capacity for the internal far-from-equilibrium conditions to be prompted by a new type of environmental contact.

This is not just a semantical quibble about the differences between open and closed systems. There are important practical consequences. In self-organized systems, boundaries define the identity of a system which enables it to explore its own creative resources when the environment challenges it. Gareth Morgan has pointed out how the open systems viewpoint has blinded us to recognizing systems as entities with a unique identity.[5] This identity, which boundaries largely determine, is not just a reaction to its environment, it is, so to speak, *enacting* its environment. For example, organizations don't just react to markets, they can also create new markets through advertising, distribution of their product, sales strategies, and so on. Boundaries establish system identities, and the identity demarcates the approach the system takes to the environment.

Thus, boundaries correct a viewpoint that is too open in the open systems model. A crucial role of boundaries, therefore, is to put the onus back on the system and its resources to be more than a mechanism that merely reacts to environmental variation. Self-organization, after all, is the system's creative response to the challenge that originates in the environment; it is not a blind reaction like a force acting on the content of a force-field. In fact, in Lewin's linear and equilibrium-based force-field model, the field is not a bounded system at all.

Going back to the Benard system for a moment—the glass vessel provides a bounded region that contains the amplification of the random currents. Without this bounded region, the amplification would explode, breach the boundary, and destroy the system. In self-organization, boundaries contain and fix the nonlinear process of self-organization. In human systems, *boundaries provide a safe holding environment* for anxiety and other uncomfortable experiences that accompany the emergence of novelty under a far-from-equilibrium condition. Boundaries keep anxiety from becoming counterproductive. In other words, firm boundaries allow far-from-equilibrium challenges to remain challenges, not threats.

Creating a Safe, Bounded Arena for Change

Hirschhorn offers another example of how organizational change requires boundaries.[6] In a change project involving the mayor of a large city and his cabinet, there was tension between the mayor's central staff and the commissioners who headed up the different city agencies. In designing a retreat, the consultant faced a choice: should the groups be divided into homogeneous or heterogeneous subgroups? Homogeneous subgroups would separate the central staff and the commissioners into two groups respectively. Heterogeneous groups, on the other hand, would mix the members.

The decisions was to start the process out with heterogeneous groups since this would be a safer bounded arena than having two homogeneous groups with a history of hostility. On the second day, however, once a sense of security was more firmly established, homogeneous groups were formed to confront more directly the existing tension. The result was that now, in this bounded, safe arena, real transformation had a chance to take place.

The approach to organizational change advocated in this book is not about destroying boundaries, and, thereby, creating a paralyzing sense of insecurity. Instead, I'm advocating that firming boundaries must take place contiguously with work on traversing boundaries to connect the system to the environment. Challenging the system into a far-from-equilibrium condition and working on boundaries go hand and hand.

TRAVERSING BOUNDARIES: CONTACT WITH THE ENVIRONMENT

To bring about self-organization, organizational boundaries need to be firmed-up as well as breached. Once there is some modicum of a bounded system, the system can be connecting to its environment.

Chapters 4 and 5 indicated how systems dominated by equilibrium-seeking processes function as *isolated* systems—their boundaries are not permeable to new information or to a vital exchange with their environments. In an organizational context this indicates that self-fulfilling prophecies are maintaining the equilibrium and creating a recursive cycle that is information-tight and environmentally closed. In Chapter 5 we gave the example of a typewriter manufacturer, whose self-enclosed sense of identity was supported and reinforced by a self-fulfilling prophecy, and was, accordingly, not open to the environmental information that word-processing was taking over the market.

In the Benard system self-organization takes place when a far-from-equilibrium condition pushes the liquid system out of its isolated status. That is, the robust exchange of heat from the Benard system's environment sets up the far-from-equilibrium conditions necessary for self-organization.

The fact that the Benard system is now in a robust exchange with its environment does not mean that the boundary that separates the system from the environment has disappeared. The vessel that holds the liquid is still there, but the vessel has become permeable to the exchange of heat. On the one hand, if the vessel were made of a non-heat-conducting material, then the system would remain isolated and the boundary would act as an impermeable shield. On the other hand, if the vessel were too permeable the liquid would just leak out, and there would no longer be a Benard system. Thus, the boundary between the system and its environment must be permeable enough to allow an energy exchange, but not so permeable that it destroys the distinction between the system and the environment.

CONNECTING SYSTEMS AND ENVIRONMENTS IN ORGANIZATIONS

Environments can be internal and external. The external dimension includes:

- customers and market

- government regulators, who monitor various aspects of the organization's operations, such as OSHA, Department of Labor and Bureau of Labor Statistics, EEOC, Office of Federal Contract Compliance, Joint Commission on Accreditation of Healthcare Organizations, and so on

- suppliers of raw materials

- other organizations involved in joint ventures, associations, etc.

- similar companies with whom vital information is being exchanged

The internal environments of work groups would include:

- other work groups that send or receive work, internal staff functions such as Human Resources, Accounting and Budgeting, and so on

- other organizational groups involved in any important way in the work the group is doing

Again, when equilibrium-seeking dominates a system, the organization or work group is too shielded from these environments, whether internal or external. A far-from-equilibrium condition can, therefore, be generated by connecting a system with an environment from which it was previously isolated. Coupling a system to an environment, therefore, is one way to facilitate organizational transformation. This explains why the commonsensical "being close to your customer" has been so powerful in eliciting organizational improvement. The contact with the environment can aid in the generation of a far-from-equilibrium condition and release the potential for change that is locked up in the nonlinear system. This means that a significant role for a change agent or manager is in facilitating this connection between a work group or organization and its environment.

It needs to be pointed out, however, that facilitating environmental contact does not consist in merely adapting to current environments. Systems also can be involved in creating new environments with whom they are in vital contact. Consider, for example, a baby at the stage of learning to walk. Walking introduces a connection to a new environmental arena for the child, that is, the areas that can be circumambulated by walking and not merely by crawling. The walking baby is now living in a different world, a world reached by walking. Thus, development implies that a new capacity opens up a new environmental arena wherein that capacity is exercised. The far-from-equilibrium conditions that promote growth and change are also about the creative opening of new environments for work groups and organizations.

To see the importance of traversing boundaries and connecting a system to its environment, let's take a look, first, at an example of a failure to connect a system to its environment during an organizational change effort. After that we will turn to an organization that successfully promoted transformation by connecting intensely to its environments.

Work Group Isolation at "North Lake Hospital"

The Head Nurse of a neurological nursing unit at "North Lake Hospital," a prestigious teaching hospital in a suburban community in the Northeast, had an exceptional insight: many patients on her unit, who were dependent on ventilators for their breathing, did not require intensive medical care; rather, all they needed was intensive nursing care. Therefore, if these patients could receive adequate nursing care on a floor like hers, they needn't be sent to the Intensive Care Unit. This would benefit the hospital by cutting down on patient care demands facing the ICU. It would also benefit her floor by upgrading the level of nursing care.

Because ventilator-dependent patients require special rooms, as well as improved patient/nurse ratio, it would be necessary to create a special subunit on the floor: an Intensive Nursing Unit (INU). This would significantly change how things were done on the floor.

Being a very skilled administrator and having commitment to planned organizational change, the Head Nurse initiated the change project by having planning sessions with her staff to get them ready for the change. Her plan included the following elements:

- Divide the change project into four areas, for which the Head Nurse and three Assistant Head Nurses would be responsible: physical environment; education; administrative; and, documentation.

- Establish a pilot program of an INU in one room with two semi-private beds. The pilot would require additional staffing to have the appropriate nurse—patient ratio for intensive nursing care. This, of course, would require support from "North Lake's" Nursing Administration.

- Elicit support from the Nursing Education Department, since education was one of the biggest pieces.

- Involve "North Lake's" CEO, who wanted to solve the problem of excessive demand for the ICU. (Also, the Head Nurse believed her final plan of clusters of INUs on each floor would surely get the CEO to buy into the new program, because it would free up beds all over the hospital.)

- Anticipate the resistance of the 48 staff nurses on the floor. Make them ready for the change, by selling the idea to all three shifts. It was pointed out that nursing staff participation would be used in the development of patient criteria, i.e., which patients would be accepted onto the INU, as well as in determining room supplies.

Certainly, this plan was well thought out and the change intervention went ahead smoothly due to the adroitness of the Head Nurse. Nursing management, including the Director of Nursing, gave their support. Nursing Education developed specially tailored in-service education programs on caring for the ventilator-dependent patient. The CEO, excited because something was to be done to cut down on ICU usage, got involved on-site in designing the physical environment of the new rooms. Even the physicians supported it, not an easy thing to accomplish for a nurse-inspired program!

As anticipated, the staff nurses indeed resisted. They knew it wouldn't work. They said it would cause increase in turnover and burn-out. The Head Nurse was quite adept at dealing with this resistance—the project was introduced to the staff nurses as a trial program that was based on an identified need for overflow patients from the Intensive Care Unit. The Head Nurse sold the benefits of the program by pointing out how the INU concept would help the staff nurses upgrade their skill levels and make them more marketable. The Head Nurse also assured them that if the concept was shown to be valid, they would get all the staff support they needed for getting through the three months.

As can be seen, everything for excellent change management was present: top management commitment, education, staff participation, planning, and overcoming resistance to change. Indeed, the first patient arrived soon after the room was prepared, and after a month, another patient entered the INU. The nurses began to love working there, and their skills were becoming honed enough that after only eight weeks, they didn't need any extra help from clinical educators. At twelve weeks it was running so well that the INU took on a third patient.

Yet with all that, the program eventually fell on its face. Extra staff support was withdrawn at twelve weeks into the program. Shortly there-after, the whole INU came to a screeching stop as the Head Nurse had to halt it due to lack of staff.

In terms of the traditional model of change the problem was traced to one cause: the withdrawal of top management support for the extra staff needed. "Can't afford it." In terms of the linear and equilibrium model, this meant that one of the main forces imposed on the system to get it moving toward change was taken away. Or, in Lewinian terminology, the new, changed conditions were refrozen enough. The additional staff was to have buttressed the changed conditions. When the buttress collapsed, the program collapsed.

From the point of view of self-organization, however, a question must be asked: Were the organizational boundaries traversed enough to generate the requisite far-from-equilibrium conditions? It seems the nursing unit, even the whole medical center, remained isolated within the shell of its own equilibrium-inducing, self-fulfilling prophecies. These self-fulfilling prophecies formed an information-tight shield between the system and its internal and external environments. This was the source of the resistance from both nurses and the administrators. No matter how much Lewinian refreezing took place, self-organization was prevented because equilibrium-maintaining isolation held sway.

Connecting System and Environment at Harley-Davidson

Harley-Davidson had a very different experience of organizational change. The company managed to traverse its boundaries and create a series of vital exchanges with its environments. The point is not to criticize the Head Nurse in the previous account and praise the management at Harley-Davidson; The two situations are vastly different. Harley-Davidson was propelled into its new way of running its business by a crisis that threatened to bankrupt the company, whereas no similar crisis occurred on the INU at "North Lake Hospital."

The popular story of what happened at Harley-Davidson Motorcycles is a good illustration of how a new and revitalized environmental contact induced far-from-equilibrium conditions that helped an organization.[6] In 1980, the quality of Harley-Davidson motorcycles was so poor that dealers actually had to place cardboard beneath the bikes to protect the showroom floor from leaking fluids. Japanese-manufactured motorcycles were taking over a huge share of the market. Harley-Davidson had to change.

One way was to connect the people in the factory who made the bikes to the people in the environment who bought the bikes. Harley-Davidson invited customers in to explain what they liked and didn't like about the bikes and to point out mechanical problems. This connection of employees to customers was a radical move: the inner system was put in vital contact with the external environment.

As a result, along with this new environmental contact, came other significant changes. Quality shot way up, and Harley-Davidson began to forge a renewed reputation for high-quality bikes. Again, the company moved away from equilibrium, away from a tendency just to keep doing what already was done by maintaining the old system/environment contact the way it had always been.

Harley-Davidson also revitalized or created anew many other system/environmental connections that offered extremely valuable sources for two-way exchanges of information. First, purchasers of motorcycles enroll free for the first year in owner's clubs. These clubs give the new owners friends to ride with and sponsor periodic rallies. The internal group directors of the owner's clubs oversee local and regional chapters. For Harley-Davidson itself, these clubs are a phenomenal source of information, and a huge data-base is kept on them.

Second, Harley-Davidson and the owner clubs sponsor many "hog" rallies 35 weeks of the year. These rallies are not only attended by the bikers, but by Harley's top management as well. They interact with customers, mechanics, dealers, and Harley production people, and ride the bikes themselves.

Third, whereas in the past a prospective customer could only take a demo ride on the company's oval track, now Harley-Davidson has marked a 9- to 16-mile track on local roads. The customer is given the keys and turned loose, with the request, "Please bring it back." When they return, a Harley representative meets with them and asks about their impressions.

Finally, other system/environment interactions include an extensive dealer network, customer satisfaction surveys, vital associations with suppliers, and so on. All of these system/environment connections expedited such a successful organizational transformation that, in Japan, where there are a host of state-of-the-art, high-tech motorcycles being manufactured, the Japanese are gobbling up Harleys. Once the paradoxical work on boundaries is underway, the far-from-equilibrium conditions prompting self-organization can be initiated.

DIFFERENCES THAT MAKE
A DIFFERENCE

The image of Community.
Thus the sage organizes the people
And makes distinctions between things.
—I CHING (HEXAGRAM 13)

We hear a great deal lately about the need for the modern organization to encourage consensus-seeking, team-building, conflict resolution. Indeed, on first impression they sound constructive, especially if we have experienced organizations fraught with destructive conflict, little sharing of authority, and distracting competition. So let's find ways of aligning people behind common organizational goals; of establishing ways of working that encourage esprit de corps and a sense of teamwork that expand our ability to coordinate the multifarious tasks we need to do as our work environments grow more complex.

We need to be careful though, that we are not simply imposing a participative corporate culture on what was previously not a teamwork environment.

Real teams emerge out of the process of self-organization. To be sure, the emergence of greater coordination and coherence in a system is similar to cohesive teamwork. A close look at self-organization, though, reveals that emergent coherence is not based on a premature consensus among the parts of a system, but is, instead, the result of the amplification of *differences* in the system. Consider, for a moment, the following example of an organizational change project that used a typical method to eliminate differences.

SURVEY FEEDBACK MAINTAINS EQUILIBRIUM
AT "MIDWEST INSTITUTE"

As a preliminary step in implementing a TQM program at a large educational research facility, "Midwest Institute," the steering committee filled out a survey of management practices. The questions were formatted with a typical numerical scale from 1 through 5, where 1 stood for definitely agree and 5 stood for definitely disagree. The group decided to average their scores, believing this would make it easier to understand the results. Averaging is a customary technique in survey feedback that represents a consensus of the work group's perceptions and collapses cumbersome data into a more usable form.

Notice, however, that averaging obliterates differences in individual responses. For example, one of the survey questions was:

My manager always encourages suggestions to improve work methods:

definitely agree			definitely disagree	
1	2	3	4	5

In response to this question:

one person selected 1
two persons selected 2
one person selected 4
one person selected 5

The average of these scores is 2.8, very near the middle. But feeding back 2.8 does not include the wide variance found in the actual responses. This means the potential information inherent in the original responses has degenerated, a process equivalent to a system eliminating departures from equilibrium. Averaging substitutes an idealized mathematical norm for the real, complex relationships in the group, and as a result, it is data, not information, that is fed back. Allowing the group to mistake data for real information actually impedes the flow of information. Since no new information is being generated, the work unit remains under the sway of equilibrium.

Of course, fancier statistics could have been used, such as standard deviations, variances, and so on. But, even in that form the actual differences among the members would be downplayed to how each member's score differs from the mean. This is not to criticize statistics, but to point out that efforts during organizational change often do not enrich, but decrease, the power of information, and, consequently, does not facilitate a far-from-equilibrium condition. Any intervention that subjugates individual differences results in decreasing information and reinforcing equilibrium, whether the intervention is premature consensus-seeking, or the imposition of participative structures.

DIFFERENCE QUESTIONING

INFORMATION AS A DIFFERENCE THAT MAKES A DIFFERENCE

Now that we have seen an example of what does not work in facilitating the generation of information in a system, we need to address the question of what does work. As pointed out in Chapter 6, if equilibrium and new information are incompatible, then ways of increasing information in an organization or work group are equivalent to the setting-up of a far-from-equilibrium condition. Generating information to establish a far-from-equilibrium condition challenges the work group or organization to self-organize and transform itself.

In order to better grasp exactly what's involved in generating information to establish a far-from-equilibrium condition, let's look closer at the role of information in a social system like an organization. The late polymath Gregory Bateson viewed information as the crucial commodity of exchange in a social system and understood a *bit of information* as a difference that makes a difference.[1] That is, information is what the members of a social system process in all their significant dealings with one another. Again, we can use the analogy of a room with a thermostat regulating its temperature. Information is the difference the system senses between the actual temperature and the preset range. This vital difference activates the thermostat to turn heating and cooling mechanisms on or off.

In an organization, we constantly monitor and act on differences; for example, between current inventory levels and customer demands, between quality standards and the current status of our product or service, between the skill levels of different employees, and so on. Of course, as stated previously, the traditional role of a manager is to notice such differences, and control them by eliminating them.

In their need to understand how families can change to become more functional, family systems theorists refined Bateson's understanding of information into "news of a relationship difference" in the family.[2] Differences in social/family relationships, and how these relationships are perceived by the members is equivalent to information in the system. Information, then, comes from elaborating on differences among the members of a social group in terms of how they see what is going on, how they experience their involvement in the social system, and how they interact with other members. Consequently, an increase in information in a group or organization is an increase in the knowledge available to the system concerning its own functioning.

THE SELF-GENERATION OF INFORMATION

If, as Bateson put it, information is a difference that makes a difference, then generating a far-from-equilibrium condition is a matter of *generating differences that make a difference* in an organization or work group. This entails, however, that this making a difference is not dampened by the equilibrium-seeking tendencies in the group. For example, imposing information only activates equilibrium-seeking tendencies that provoke the group into resisting the information. Of course, this is what the self-fulfilling prophecy does in its penchant for blocking new information in a group.

The key for generating differences that make a difference must be to create conditions under which information is *self-generated*. The challenge that faces facilitators of organizational change is to find what expedites the work group or organization to generate new information internally.

A far-from-equilibrium condition activates a system's nonlinearity to bring about self-organization. The information that the system generates must concern the self-fulfilling prophecies that reinforce the equilibrium condition. The organization must generate its own information around its self-fulfilling aspects.

DIFFERENCE QUESTIONING TO CHANGE FAMILY SYSTEMS

A technique that work groups and organizations can use to generate new information is *difference questioning*. This technique was first developed to facilitate change in family systems.[3] Difference questioning dislodges the stuck patterns of dysfunctional families in which there is pressure for members to conform to a certain picture of what the family is all about. Confronting this conformist tendency, difference questioning can evoke differences in viewpoint among the members of the social group, and thereby, interrupt the equilibrium-seeking propensity of the system by showing how everyone does not agree with this picture. In other words, difference questioning is *non*-consensus-seeking because it highlights the differences among members' viewpoints.

The family therapist as system change agent asks questions that elicit a difference in the family system. For example, the mother in the family might state she is angry. This statement by itself is only data and, as such, has little power to unleash change. By difference questioning, however, the therapist might ask the other members of the family to rate the mother's anger when one of the siblings comes home late. Their answers are new information available to the family system about how each member's perceptions compare with the other members. This new information is new knowledge available to the system about its internal patterns of relationships.

Difference questioning works to bring about a far-from-equilibrium condition when it is applied to those areas of the family's functioning that keep the family in an equilibrium condition. We can see how difference questioning can interrupt equilibrium in another example from a family whose equilibrium centered around the problem of a hyperactive child.[4] We'll call the child John, and his two siblings, Mary and Bill. A self-fulfilling prophecy linked the family's expectations about the behavior of the child, the accompanying belief that the family's problems were all derived from this behavior, and the actual hyperactive behavior that confirmed the original beliefs and expectations. Difference questioning interrupted this vicious circle by introducing new information about the relationships and perceptions of the family members. Examples of such questions were: Who was most hyper or jittery before John became hyper, Bill or Mary? If John becomes less hyper, who will be most cooperative in the future, Mary or Bill? Which of you, Mom or Dad, is most attentive to John when he is acting hyper? And so on.

Eliciting such differences makes a difference by introducing new information into the group. This information is not available when the equilibrium-seeking tendency of the group collapses individual differences into conformity. Consequently, by difference questioning, the system generates a far-from-equilibrium condition. This challenge prompts the system to reorganize its fundamental structures and patterns of relationships.

The equilibrium-seeking, self-fulfilling areas are precisely those areas in the system that are the nodal points of resistance to change. As we indicated in Chapters 4 and 5, the nodal points of resistance also contain the hidden nodal points of change, where the equilibrium conditions mask the underlying nonlinearity in the system. Difference questioning targets these points of greatest information encapsulation. Since equilibrium is a state of low information, when the system can generate new information about its own organization or patterns of relationship then it is moving beyond equilibrium. As new information accumulates, the family can no longer continue to function (or, more precisely, dysfunction) the way it used to.

Similar to the way heat creates an internal temperature and density difference in the Benard liquid, which challenges it to self-organize, the generation of new information in the family challenges the system to reorganize itself spontaneously to deal more effectively with the new information. This is the origin of the self-organizing transformation that may take place as the family moves from a dysfunctional to a more functional way of being organized.

DIFFERENCE QUESTIONING IN ORGANIZATIONS AND WORK GROUPS

In organizational settings, difference questioning can generate creative comparisons of each individual's perspective on what is going on. This adds knowledge to the group about how the parts of the system are interrelated. As the information circulates in the group, small departures from group norms that once had negligible effects due to the tendency of equilibrium-seeking, are now permitted and encouraged. The eventual outcome is that the group is primed to take advantage of and to use departures from equilibrium to formulate new directions, strategies, and other creative alternatives in its functioning.

How to Generate Information, Not Data

An increase in information, not data, expedites far-from-equilibrium conditions in organizations. In a work setting, for example, instead of the data announcement "I am tired," the information announcement would take this data and expand it to: "I am tired because I have been working my buns off for two weeks on this project," while a co-worker's response might be "I am not tired, because I'm working on a different project and I've had a chance to play a lot of golf this week."

The point here is not to place value judgments on each person's behavior, but to highlight the differences between their perceptions and experiences of the work situation. This example may seem to be about a trivial matter, however, it is not trivial that there is a *difference* in perception between these two group members. This difference was probably downplayed in the group's tendency toward conformity. The differences elicited introduce more information into the social system. The very discrepancy between their responses generates that new information.

Another example that shows the difference between information and mere data is the all-important organizational chart. As presented in its visual form, such a chart, which describes the managerial hierarchy, is mere data. Difference questioning regarding this hierarchy elicits information that concerns how each member in the organization describes his or her view of how persons listed in that chart are related to one another organizationally. Probing these differences in perception would surely reveal something about the pattern of relationships in the system.

Difference Questioning Undermines Self-Fulfilling Prophecies

Difference questioning facilitates far-from-equilibrium conditions when the questions focus on those organizational areas in which self-fulfilling prophecies keep the organization in a no-change situation. Chapter 5 described five types of self-fulfilling structures that maintain equilibrium and resist change. Directing questions about differences at equilibrium-maintaining processes frees the system from equilibrium dominance.

Therefore, difference questioning aims at increasing information around expectations, beliefs, attitudes, and behaviors that keep the work group or organization from changing. Let's take a look at how this can be done.

Difference Questioning at "Parkside Hospital"

We need to revisit the courtesy program that was so poorly received by clerks at "Parkside Hospital" (see Chapter 4). Their resistance to the program is a perfect opportunity to question differences, since this resistance can be interpreted as a self-fulfilling prophecy that reinforced the equilibrium-seeking tendency of the group.

First, we need to keep in mind that difference questioning does not include imposing different attitudes that someone else, such as the manager, may want the group to have. Rather, the group itself generates information about its self-fulfilling cycles of attitude, behavior, and results. The operating assumption here is that the ward clerks' current discourteous responses, both to staff, patients, and patients' families and to the training program, are a manifestation of a self-fulfilling, equilibrium-seeking process. The abrupt, snappy, and nasty attitudes and behaviors of these employees are tied in to the survival of these ward clerks in their organizational system.

Therefore, to facilitate difference questioning in this situation, the training program is put on the back burner, and questions are initiated by interviewing the ward clerks in a group setting. Questions can be asked about attitudes the different members have concerning their guests. For example, one of the floor secretaries could be asked these questions:

- What kind of patients do you find most difficult?

- How does this type of patient affect you personally?

- How do you respond?

- How is this a stressful situation for you?

- How do you deal with this stress?

Other questions asked could concern the ward clerks' responses to the other people with whom they interacted—nurses, doctors, patient families, etc. These same questions are then directed toward other floor secretaries to elicit their unique perspective. Contrasts in viewpoints are highlighted.

Questions about differences can extend even further in eliciting group differences. When one employee says that egotistical doctors really get her gander, we can ask another employees for their response to such doctors, and we can even ask them to rate the intensity of their response in relation to the first person's answer. This is the opposite to the consensus-seeking that "Midwest Institute" aimed for by averaging group response in the example with which we opened the chapter.

Someone might claim at this juncture, "Hey, we're not doing family therapy with these employees—they have a job to do and we want them to do it better!" This is correct, but only up to a point. Certainly, change agents are not doing family therapy with employees, but they are facilitating self-organization, which represents a transformation in the work system. If this transformation is to be genuine, then self-organization presents a more appropriate way of transformation than the mere shift in equilibrium levels that is the legacy of the traditional approach. If transformation is what an organization wants, then self-organization is the way, and difference questioning is one way of facilitating the far-from-equilibrium conditions necessary for self-organization.

At "Parkside Hospital" one of the outcomes of difference questioning was the group's insight that the self-fulfilling prophecy reinforced their discourteous behavior because of the intense level of stress of their jobs. Stress seemed to be so central and relentless, that they feared any change would make their jobs even more stressful. The new training program was viewed as change and therefore, had to be resisted.

Eventually, instead of continuing the courtesy program as originally planned, the floor secretaries worked with a consultant, to create a stress-management program that focused on ways they could reduce stress and feel better when they encountered the patients, nurses, and doctors. This stress-management program was a spontaneous, self-organizing phenomenon that eventually led to a transformation in their behaviors. This unexpected, self-generated emergence of this program changed their behavior far more profoundly than a courtesy-training program.

Differences generate and free energy that is bound up in self-fulfilling, equilibrium-seeking tendencies. Therefore, anything that can generate information in and around a self-fulfilling prophecy can induce a far-from-equilibrium condition. Difference questioning truly draws out this kind of information and facilitates a far-from-equilibrium condition that prompts self-organization. When organizational change interventions work, it is likely that the change agents and members of the group are eliciting information, even if these explicit terms are not used.

It is crucial to point out that this difference questioning differs from manipulating resistance. The focus shifts from how to overcome resistance to how resistance can be a source of valuable information that the group can use to find alternative ways of functioning. Indeed, originally, the hospital attempted to manipulate the ward clerks' resistance by selling them on how the courtesy-training program would benefit them by having more patients return to the hospital, which would improve the hospital's finances and so on. But this information was not self-generated, because it had nothing to do with the way the ward clerks had organized their system. Information, after all, ultimately has to do with knowledge that is available to the system about its own way of functioning. Manipulation cannot evoke such knowledge, but difference questioning might.

CULTURAL DIFFERENCE QUESTIONING

Difference questioning can also be a vehicle for change in the emerging multicultural work force.[5] Instead of fearing that cultural diversity might increase conflict in the work place, we can recognize the potential for diversity to be a source of creativity, innovation, and intercultural understanding. These qualities can be extremely valuable vehicles for organizational change.

At first sight, questioning cultural differences may seem to go against the grain of guidelines of EEO and Affirmative Action. Anti-discrimination policies and practices have inculcated a philosophy that suggests that cultural issues are not to be touched, and, therefore, cultural differences are to be deemphasized. Ignoring differences, however, denies how employee self-esteem, confidence, and security are powerfully rooted in ethnic and cultural identity. Research in the social sciences has demonstrated over and over again that our ethnic and cultural identification is so strong that it is misleading to say that culture influences our personality, for this implies that culture is external to and acting on our personality. Instead, who we are is equivalent partly to being a member of a certain cultural group, and our cultural group is defined by its difference from other cultural identities. Therefore, glossing over our cultural identification is tantamount to ignoring us as individuals.

Instead, by questioning cultural differences we recognize and respect cultural differences. We expand the concept of fair treatment

so that through recognizing differences *we treat people as they want to be treated in terms of their cultural identification, to the extent that it's practical and healthy for individuals and the organization.* Cultural, ethnic, and racial differences are, therefore, brought to the surface, discussed, and explored. This notion seems so fraught with potentials for misuse that when these ideas were first expounded in an article, the editors of the journal found it necessary to attach a legal disclaimer!

CULTURAL DIFFERENCE QUESTIONING AT "METRO CITY CENTRAL WAREHOUSE AND STORAGE"

At the shipping desk in "Metro City Central Warehouse and Storage," the inventory supervisor and the shipping supervisor were often in conflict over which department got an order wrong. In fact, the history of such altercations throughout this culturally diverse organization was longstanding. The shipping supervisor is from the west side of Chicago; his parents are first-generation Polish immigrants. The inventory supervisor is a Black Caribbean from the Grenadines who came to the United States when he was 17.

In the past, their manager followed EEO guidelines and believed that prying into cultural backgrounds would only open a Pandora's box of discrimination issues. Therefore, she attributed this and similar conflicts to a personality clash. This downplay of differences is equivalent to the dominance of equilibrium in a system. Hence, questioning cultural differences goes right to heart of the equilibrium-seeking process by evoking the obvious cultural differences. Because this process puts the onus of discovery about cultural differences onto the participants in the conflict, the manager's role is that of a facilitator who guides a discussion that brings cultural differences to the surface.

Here are the suggested steps of the process:

Identify cultural "hot buttons." At this stage attempt to discover the underlying cultural differences that are at the root of the conflict. For example, at "Metro City Central," the manager and changer could probe the two parties for the specific things that set each other off. On the one hand, the shipping supervisor may say that the inventory supervisor comes around with an attitude in which he demands respect and appreciation for doing just what's expected of him and his department. On the other hand, the inventory supervisor may say that the shipping supervisor is quick to blame the inventory department whenever there's a problem.

By finding these "hot buttons," those involved can then relate them to the different cultural backgrounds of each party.

Look for the cultural source. At this stage, participants connect the hot button to the different backgrounds of each party. Note that the connection is not imposed on the people involved—instead, each person comes up with the cultural differences on his or her own. The manager or change agent, however, may have a notion about this cultural connection, so it's okay to state this connection as a possibility if the employees have not been able to make a cultural linkage to their hot button. But, the manager should make this connection only by suggesting it and asking for feedback about the correctness of his or her supposition.

For example, the manager could follow through on a cultural remark by asking, "Was this idea about people demanding respect for just doing what's expected an issue where you grew up?" Here is where cultural differences about values and attitudes surface. The shipping supervisor may reveal that in his Polish neighborhood respect was something that people had to earn—doing what was expected wasn't good

Questioning Cultural Differences as Preventive Maintenance

Cultural difference questioning can be a powerful vehicle for change, even before explicit conflict breaks out. Have a work group fill out the following cultural difference survey, and then use the results as stepping stones into a discussion on cultural differences. This can accomplish several things at once:

• Legitimize cultural differences as a healthy fact about workplace diversity.
• Open for discussion the whole arena of cultural differences.
• Build awareness that cultural differences may underlie conflicts at work.
• Develop teams around collaborative problem-solving to resolve differences based in culture, ethnic background, race, or gender.

It is extremely important to point out that the cultural difference survey is not tabulated by averages. Instead, diversity of response reflects diversity of culture in the work group. The discussion gives the work-group members an opportunity to see how widely these attitudes or values may differ.

Cultural Difference Survey: "Where I Come From..."
INSTRUCTIONS:

First, read the value statements below. Consider each statement from the standpoint of your upbringing by ranking them on the following scale:

1 (deeply held)　　　3 (neutral)　　　5 (deeply reject)

1. Authority must be respected above all else.
1　　　2　　　3　　　4　　　5
2. Self-reliance is more important than group support.
1　　　2　　　3　　　4　　　5
3. Everyone is equal.
1　　　2　　　3　　　4　　　5
4. Being loyal to your friends overrides personal safety.
1　　　2　　　3　　　4　　　5
5. With enough determination and ambition anyone can become a success.
1　　　2　　　3　　　4　　　5
6. One should never order around another person.
1　　　2　　　3　　　4　　　5
7. Most people get what they deserve.
1　　　2　　　3　　　4　　　5
8. The purpose of life is to enjoy yourself as much as possible.
1　　　2　　　3　　　4　　　5
9. Respecting others is less important than respecting yourself.
1　　　2　　　3　　　4　　　5
10. Open conflict should be avoided at all costs.
1　　　2　　　3　　　4　　　5

enough. Moreover, awaiting respect that is not earned was an insult to the person who was giving the respect. The inventory supervisor might say that in the culture of his Caribbean island, respect was a given; it was assumed during social interaction. Furthermore, in his country, people just don't blame others immediately for mistakes. A lot of tact and diplomacy go into finding out what went wrong.

Summarize the conflict as a cultural difference. Here, the manager explicitly links the conflict to the respective cultural, ethnic, or racial backgrounds of the parties. Again, the manager phrases it as a question, so the employees can both verify the linkage, as well as clarify the specific cultural values or attitudes he or she is carrying around. In our example, the manager takes what both parties say about their cultures and summarizes it as two sets of cultural values or attitudes about respect and mistake correction. Then she checks back with each person to make sure that the summary doesn't contain distortions or misunderstandings. This also gives the participants another opportunity to express the attitudes and values of their cultures.

Recognizing that cultural differences can influence a conflict allows the parties to work together to come up with ways of keeping intercultural difference from interfering with work.

PURPOSE CONTRASTING

Self-fulfilling prophecies isolate a system and keep it information-tight. The original expectation or attitude creates a loop of belief and action that is self-confirming and, therefore, information-tight. An organization's or work group's sense of its purpose can be one type of the expectation phase of a self-fulfilling prophecy. This purpose then leads to behaviors that serve to confirm it.

For example, a work group in an insurance company may have a sense of its purpose in processing medical insurance claims. The insurance work unit receives the claim, (the raw material) from one of its environments, (the person covered by the policy) then processes the claim, and eventually pays the hospital and the client, two other environments of the company.

Obviously, the original purpose of any work group or organization is to accomplish its work, which is to provide a product or service to an environment (a client). When everything runs smoothly, then the sense of purpose leads to appropriate actions, and there is an appropriate exchange with the environments, that is, the purpose of the work is accomplished.

Problems arise when the original purpose of environmental exchange is eclipsed. Of course, this is a well-known phenomenon in bureaucracies, which have been criticized for encouraging the purpose to shift from environmental exchange to maintaining their own existence. Indeed, we can question the true purpose of large corporations: Is it to exchange a product or service with customers or to keep the executives in the standard of living to which they have become accustomed?

Sometimes, the very need to survive obscures the original purpose. In a difficult environment, a work group, or even an entire organization, can develop an enclosed, protective mechanism, a self-fulfilling, information-tight enclosure that keeps environmental exchange to a minimum. Seeking to survive then becomes the dominant factor in the system, overriding its original purpose. And, of course, that is when organizational transformation becomes especially important.

In the model of change as self-organization, purpose contrasting can generate information that sparks a transformation of the organization. Again, the emphasis is on creating new information in the system, and, again, this occurs through questioning and recognizing differences. In this case, the organization needs to evoke the difference between its original purpose and the current purpose. Contrasting the current and the original purpose generates a difference, and introduces new information into the group.[6] By highlighting these differences, the organization's new way of reaching it's original purpose emerges in the self-organization that is triggered.

PURPOSE CONTRASTING AT "PARKSIDE HOSPITAL"

Returning to the situation at "Parkside Hospital," the ward clerks operated under the purpose of survival, which had evolved in the hostile environment they faced in their jobs at the low end of the pecking order. They were in positions where they were subjected to the intense stress endemic in the health care setting. Let's face it: except for mothers giving birth, none of the other patients wanted to be in the hospital.

The ward clerk's function is to act as the hub of this stressful system. To be sure, the original purpose of the ward clerks was not abetted by the behavior and attitudes that alienated the hospital's guests, whether internal or external. Yet, through years of somehow getting the job done, at least to a minimum degree, a new purpose of survival emerged that led to behaviors perceived as abrupt, snappy, or nasty. The less-than-nice response to such behaviors on the part of the guests would, of course, confirm the ward clerks' original expectation of a hostile and threatening environment. Therefore, the behaviors they practiced were appropriate in context. Hence, the self-fulfilling nature of the system and the hostile environment led to the emergence of the purpose of survival.

The ward clerks needed to examine the contrast between their current purpose of survival and their original purpose to provide a viable conduit for the various activities in a nursing unit. This could be done in a group setting, with a facilitator difference questioning, directing the inquiry with such questions as:

- What are you supposed to accomplish around here?

- How do you know when you have accomplished your purpose effectively?

- What do you spend most of your energy and attention on?

- Who are your clients and what are you expected to do for them?

- What do your expect from your environment?

- What are your behaviors in relation to these expectations?

- What have you been doing in order to survive?

- What do you need in order to survive even better?

Holding this contrast and examining it generates information, it is a far-from-equilibrium condition that permits an exploration of creative alternatives for the work group to accomplish its work. Difference questioning and purpose contrasting are only two methods for generating information. The next two chapters offer more methods for challenging assumptions underlying a self-fulfilling prophecy.

9

THE CAULDRON OF CHANGE

Nothing transforms so much as the cauldron.
That which is old and useless is removed
To make room for something new
—I Ching (Hexagram 50, yin in the first line)

Far-from-equilibrium conditions guarantee that normal, equilibrium-maintaining dynamics will be disrupted. Chapter 8 described various methods for highlighting and amplifying differences to initiate far-from-equilibrium conditions. The result is an increase of information, and as information increases, a system reorganizes itself to incorporate the new information into a new manner of functioning.

This chapter continues to explore far-from-equilibrium conditions by taking a closer look at the features of those challenges that can interrupt equilibrium-seeking. A far-from-equilibrium challenge removes old patterns in order to make way for new patterns to emerge. As we have already seen, this does not occur through managerial pressure, which is counterproductive in activating the inner potential for transformation in a nonlinear system. Instead, the challenge of far-from-equilibrium conditions brings out the system's own capacity to *transform itself*.

A far-from-equilibrium challenge questions underlying assumptions within the self-fulfilling prophecy. New information can be introduced into the system if the assumptions that supported the tendency to exclude information are themselves examined. A direct questioning assault on beliefs won't work, however, because such a challenge will be rebuffed by the circular and recursive barrier inherent in the self-fulfilling prophecy. The far-from-equilibrium challenge must be designed to interrupt the interactions between beliefs, expectations, actions, and results.

139

That, of course, is the challenge for change agents: change must take place in the face of the strong hold that past norms have on the system. Indeed, OD has cultivated many techniques for changing organizational norms and bringing them to the surface. The question remains, however, whether these methods succeed in interfering with the equilibrium-seeking power of the old norms. If the transformation is truly as radical as self-organization demands, then the new norms that guide the behavior of the organization need to emerge as a result of the creative response of the group, not as the result of imposition.

Of course, the creative response of organizations to all sorts of challenges is not novel in the history of organizational change. Successful leaders, managers, and change agents have challenged organizations to change since prehistoric times. The key question, though, is: To what extent do these means of challenge actually interrupt the equilibrium-seeking dynamics of the group? In other words, what is it about a challenge that enables it to be a far-from-equilibrium challenge that prompts an organization to self-organize?

For instance, the use of survey feedback in organization development interventions is supposed to challenge a group to change. Yet, the last chapter discussed serious reservations about the efficacy of survey feedback as it is typically practiced in leading to self-organizing change. Consensus-seeking practices may simply lead to premature, equilibrium-seeking conformity, instead of challenging a group to a greater sense of creative coherence.

In the self-organization model, what makes a challenge useful in prompting self-organization is its power to interrupt what maintains the equilibrium status of the organization or work group. The right kind of challenge, directed at the right organizational practices, results in a far-from-equilibrium condition that prompts self-organization. But what are these right kinds of challenges and to what organizational practices must they be directed?

EVOKING AN ORGANIZATION'S OWN RESOURCES

Consider the example of self-organizing transformation at "Pharm-Chem," discussed in Chapter 1. The owner knew that his role in facilitating organizational transformation was to challenge the group and then leave it to them to work it out. This, of course, is what Johnsonville

Food's Ralph Stayer also eventually figured out. Inducing a far-from-equilibrium condition is not a matter of hierarchical control nor even a subtle form of it. A new kind of paradoxical control is called for, a type of control that doesn't control. This type of control consists in challenging the system, then permitting it to find its own way to self-organize.

Accordingly, the role of the change agent shifts: he or she does not bring about change. Instead, because the system itself unleashes change, the change agent's role is to make him- or herself obsolete. As Ralph Stayer realized, his role as leader was to put himself out of a job. The change agents need to turn the challenge role over to the members of the group that are involved in the change because they are the real change agents. They incorporate the challenge into the new way the system is organizing itself. This is not about building a permanent role for change agents as a way of buttressing the change process. On the contrary, initiating the right kind of challenge starts a process whereby the system, because of its nonlinearity, builds momentum that sustains the original challenge. Change agents help the system (and themselves) to get out of the way of change.

What makes a far-from-equilibrium challenge work is its utilization of the system's own natural tendencies and resources. For example, in the Benard system, the tendency of liquids to transfer heat and the capacity of the Benard liquid to form convection currents are used in the process of self-organization. A far-from-equilibrium challenge challenges a system to grapple with itself, find its own way of dealing with the challenge, and experience the freedom to self-organize in whatever manner is compatible with the challenge that faces it.

In this regard, it is important to point out that a new participative structure, by itself, is not necessarily a far-from-equilibrium challenge for organizational transformation. This is a mistake that proponents of TQM, CI, and reengineering may make. There is the belief that participative organizational structures are the utopian solution to issues of productivity and quality.

When a participative style is imposed on employees, the imposition speaks louder than the message of participation. As a result, participative structures like project teams often are simply overlaid on an organizational culture that is steeped in authoritarian, nonparticipative practices.

In the language of nonlinearity, the mere imposition of a team structure may be nothing more than a linear change in a linear system. A team structure, indeed, may not be the far-from-equilibrium match to the

Challenging Organizations Using Information Overload

We saw in the last chapter how difference questioning was one way to increase information in a system and thereby generate far-from-equilibrium conditions. There are other ways as well. For example, Margaret "Meg" Wheatley, a professor at Brigham Young University, organizational consultant, and the author of *Leadership and the New Science*, suggests a process of information overload to bring about self-organization.[1] As Wheatley puts it, in an organization "information is data interpreted into meaning because of the context of the organization. As a network of relationships, data is taken in by the organization and interpreted to become something relevant enough to notice. The relationships establish a context for taking in the data and making it meaningful."

Since information fuels self-organization, Wheatley suggests setting up conditions in a work group or organization that can generate enormous quantities of information in order to challenge the group to self-organize. At first, this generation of information takes place without specific interpretation. The participants are bombarded with facts, figures, graphs, and research that are market data for discussion. Wheatley has conducted these information overload sessions in groups of 60 to 70 people who come from all over the organization. These groups can also include customers, suppliers and other concerned outsiders.

During this process of information overload, Wheatley says the people move into a period of "intellectual chaos," which prompts them to release their preconceived notions of what the organization needs. Then, they become more open to new perspectives. In other words, information overload interrupts the equilibrium-maintaining self-fulfilling cycle and self-organization can then ensue.

Wheatley warns that consultants who facilitate such information overload retreats must be willing to encounter two possible phenomena: First, in the midst of feeling overwhelmed by the information chaos, the participants may want to fire the consultant. Second, the participants may want to limit the information field to some specific, workable area. In both cases, the facilitator needs to sustain the processes that are generating information, and of course, simultaneously keep the process within a safe and firm boundary.

system's hidden nonlinearity, and therefore, the team structure will not release the self-organizing potential of the organization or work group. Group participation indeed may have a far-from-equilibrium effect, but it may also just as easily promote *group think*, a premature consensus, in which the group as a whole sways individuals toward conformity and away from asserting their differing perspectives.

For team structures to really work in bringing about deep-rooted transformation, it is necessary for far-from-equilibrium challenges to be built into the team structure. This is what happened at "Carville General Hospital," described in Chapter 2. The TQM senior management team had established in its team charter the right to impeach the leader of the team. This is exactly what happened—the group impeached its leader, the CEO of the hospital, when he violated the team rule of coming to meetings on time. This challenge is what enabled this team to function in a truly participative culture throughout the medical center.

The rule of starting meetings on time was first adopted by a lower level group and then evolved upward to be incorporated into an upper level group. This challenge, then, was clearly not managerial imposition. Indeed, if this rule had been promulgated in the beginning of the program as a management mandate concerning all future meetings in the medical center, it most likely would not have had the effect it did.

CHALLENGING ASSUMPTIONS AT "GUIDED SYSTEMS"

Another example of how far-from-equilibrium challenges evoke a work unit's own resources in facilitating organizational change occurred at "Guided Systems," a company we first met in Chapter 3. Their great success was based on the unusually high expertise of its scientists, engineers, and technicians and its state-of-the-art technology. But, success created a self-fulfilling prophecy whereby the scientific approach to organizational direction and structure was confirmed by the development of important new products. As a result, "Guided Systems" was driven primarily by Research and Development. As competition increased in the international arena, however, "Guided Systems" had to become more market-driven. This demanded far-reaching changes in all aspects of the firm.

Three inaugurating events got the change effort off to a far-from-equilibrium start. First, mixed-process groups formed that included representatives from different functional areas who had never worked together. Design engineers and scientists sat down with production personnel, marketers, finance persons, and administrators. Before these groups even began to create a new market-driven philosophy, though, they met for three full days that were devoted to creativity practice.

Second, one of the consultants hired to guide the change process met with each of the mixed groups who then decided for themselves whether they wanted to work with him or her. This meant that change was not going to be imposed on them. Instead, a space—a "cauldron"—was created in which self-organization could take place.

Third, the change effort did not even start with the organizational assessment traditionally used for planning the intervention. As one of the consultants leading the project said, "I don't assess, because whatever picture I would get from assessment would be nothing new...and therefore, wouldn't help, because what we're after is something new. I don't want to spend time trying to swim in the mud." Therefore, instead of planning, the emphasis was on jumping right into it and working with whatever came up.

A three-day retreat was planned for each of the groups, but not focused directly on learning how to become market-oriented. Instead, the retreat emphasized creativity exercises for both individuals and the group as a whole. This was not a training program in creative problem-solving; it was a creative approach to helping the group forge a new organizational direction. Later in the chapter, we will go over the specifics of what took place in these creativity practices.

NONTHREATENING AND CREATIVE CHALLENGES

As discussed in Chapter 7, secure, firm, and safe boundaries are a prerequisite to self-organization. This needs to be kept in mind as we consider the types of challenges that can facilitate a far-from-equilibrium condition—they are not threats, but they do go right to the point where anxiety may become unmanageable. For example, John Andrews found that true learning takes place in group-process training laboratories (such as T-groups, NTL, etc.), where a basically supportive atmosphere is set up, but at the same time, individuals are placed in interpersonal situations that *disconfirm* their customary roles, attitudes, and interpersonal styles.[2] The disconfirmation facilitates a far-from-equilibrium condition by interrupting the way our normal roles, attitudes, and interpersonal styles operate as equilibrium-maintaining, self-fulfilling prophecies. The safe atmosphere of the training environment though, keeps this far-from-equilibrium-condition from becoming a threatening situation for the participants. Threats would either make people more defensive, and, therefore, reinforce the equilibrium-maintaining processes, or would lead to a sense of futility that would lead to withdrawal—hardly a condition conducive to growth and learning.

A far-from-equilibrium challenge is safe because it operates in an environment where work groups have the resources to meet the challenge. This safety has to include the security of people's jobs. Some so-called management consultants are talking nowadays about involving people in making decisions that will lead to the loss of their jobs. These same management "experts" have the gall to call this process *self-organization*, borrowing the term from the same research that is the basis of this book. It is not clear how people can be creatively challenged to reorganize their work groups when their jobs are going to be eliminated by this reorganization. But, of course, these "experts" are the same folks who refer to firing people as "redeployment" and "involuntary termination." Fancy euphemisms generate more resentment in the long run. If an organization needs to cut staff, it should call it what it is—being fired!

The purpose of a far-from-equilibrium condition that challenges assumptions is not necessarily to undermine them, but to work creatively with them. This may include strategies that seemingly depart from the original project of adding new information. For examples, creative methods may include techniques that depart from immediate assumptions. In the long run, however, this excursion does not really depart from the assumptions, it returns to the original beliefs, in terms of what underlies those beliefs. This is the essence of the creative approach—new information is generated by uncovering and questioning assumptions that underlie the beliefs that block new information. In this way an organization can harness creativity for the purpose of change.

ASSIMILATING CHALLENGES AT "CARVILLE GENERAL HOSPITAL"

To see how far-from-equilibrium challenges can become a part of the operation of an organization, we can turn back to our example of

"Carville General Hospital." In the previous authoritarian culture at the hospital, challenging each other was not part of the equilibrium and conformity-seeking pattern.

Therefore, the consultants who facilitated the team meetings had to expedite far-from-equilibrium challenges to the rigidly defined functional roles. They accomplished this by handling the differences in perspective and opinion in each team in a safe, nonthreatening manner. Team leaders were encouraged to challenge members by using their organizational roles as a justification for a position. For example, a team leader would be coached to confront a member by declaring, "We nurses won't do that!"

To make this challenge process a far-from-equilibrium condition, confrontation cannot be just a one-sided matter. Facilitators must encourage all team participants to voice their feelings in response to a challenge. The consultant modeled the original challenge from the team leader and the challenging response on the role the team member played.

Here is an example of this kind of challenge: A team member, Beth, said to another team member, Sam, "You don't seem comfortable; your arms are folded." Other members of the group protected Sam and said he was okay. The consultant intervened and turned to Sam asking how he felt about Beth confronting him. Sam said he didn't like anyone to call attention to him; he felt attacked. The consultant then asked Beth how she felt, and she replied that it took a lot of courage to say what she did, but she felt it was necessary and was disappointed that the group had not supported her. Then the consultant asked the other members how they felt and why they protected Sam. For the most part they felt bad for him, were embarrassed that Beth said it too loud, and generally wanted the whole conflict just to go away.

Next, they discussed why it was not okay to confront someone and how they could do it in a healthy way. They discussed how, in the future, their responses would include how they felt when they were challenged. By so doing, they had come up with a new rule about saying how they felt. They were now more apt to say things were not right and they could stop and discuss what was going on.

There are three ways this type of challenge helped facilitate self-organization in the team. First, the team did not try to impose a new set of norms on itself simply because some OD book said those were the right norms for participative groups. Instead, the team used their own resources to generate the new norms for challenging members. They came up with it spontaneously as their response to being challenged.

Second, the consultant's role was to encourage each team member to express how they each felt regarding the transaction that took place between Beth and Sam. This is akin to the method of difference questioning described in Chapter 8. The team generates information about its own patterns of interaction when differences are questioned.

Another way the teams experienced a challenge to their equilibrium was that at the end of each meeting time was set aside for contrasting what they thought was good about the team's performance with how they thought the team could do better. This is similar to the method of purpose contrasting also described in Chapter 8. This method highlights the difference between the original purpose and the current purpose.

FAR-FROM-EQUILIBRIUM CREATIVITY AT "GUIDED SYSTEMS"

For another look at how far-from-equilibrium challenges essentially and creatively churn up assumptions at the heart of self-fulfilling prophecies, we can turn back to "Guided Systems," where the group used creativity exercises to generate far-from-equilibrium conditions.

A three-day retreat was planned for each of the groups. The first day was spent on creative games and puzzles for individual members, as well as the group as a whole. Instead of these creativity practices being part of a general training program in creative problem-solving or idea generation, however, the games and puzzles focused on helping the group forge a new organizational direction.

The groups were asked to solve a problem that could not be solved using the traditional approach to solving engineering or scientific problems. The problems, therefore, challenged the normal habits of thinking and perception and required a radically different approach. Of course, this increased the anxiety and discomfort of the participants. Here the consultant needed to create a safe, bounded arena to contain the unpleasant feelings.

On the second day, the consultant presented various creative tools to help the participants depart from typical ruts of thought. For example, the participants practiced asking questions about the three aspects of the puzzles: the rules; the pieces; and most important, the player, that is, the "I" (see Figure 9-1).

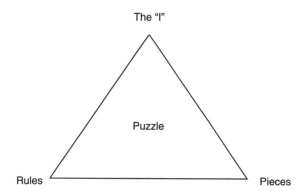

Figure 9-1. Far-From-Equilibrium Assumption Questions

Thus, by questioning the "I," the person questions his or her own tendencies toward *either/or* thinking, as well as the specific ideological prejudices that underlie his or her particular approach.

Another creativity tool they used is the word-analysis technique, which also highlights the need to depart from equilibrium. The group eventually has to redesign a cigarette box, but the approach taken to this goal is indirect. First they are asked to analyze a traffic light in terms of its shape, components, purpose, durability, and so on. In doing so, the group generates a list of 40 words that describe the traffic light. The group then applies these same 40 words to the original purpose of redesigning the cigarette box. This leads them away from being stuck in the problem and focuses them on creative approaches to solving the problem.

The first two days of the retreat had nothing to do with organizational issues. On the third day, however, the participants applied the creative process to the organizational issues at hand. This was followed up by monthly four-hour meetings. According to the consultant who headed the project, the purpose of these follow-up meetings is for "...all the time creating new meaning, and new processes."

Questioning Assumptions about Limits

Lisa Marshall of Syntax Communication Modeling Corporation offers a way of questioning that increases information in a system by focusing on specific information that is masked in over-generalized assumptions. She has incorporated this questioning method in her work with a large software firm in their development of a change management strategy. Marshall's technique looks at the filters in a firm's appraisal of its environment. In our terminology, these filters are assumptions that underlie the self-fulfilling prophecy.

Marshall suggests that this questioning process not employ the "why" question, since that often increases defensiveness, which stops the flow of information. Instead, she recommends using the more specific *what, how, who,* and *when.* Marshall's probing consists of a series of questions.

Specifying absolutes. In response to an "always" or "everybody" statement, bring it back to specific particulars. For example, in response to the statement "Everybody around here thinks that we can only hire experienced sales persons," ask: everyone? how about Jim, or Sally, or Randy? or Susan? This is similar to difference questioning since it points out differences among the perceptions of different people. Absolute thinking cuts down on information available to a system and dampens any departures from the equilibrium.

Specifying causes. Again, the emphasis is on probing into the specifics hidden in overarching explanations. For example, in response to a question about what justifies a particular course of action, the answer might be: "They (our senior managers) make us do it this way." This answer stipulates a cause-and-effect explanation for the behavior. Probing this cause and effect explanation amounts to asking, "How, specifically, do they make you do it this way?" or "Is it through a threat, reinforcement, training, role modeling...?" or "Who is it that makes you do it this way?" Again, such probing releases a great deal of information that is masked by the monolithic appearance of the cause-and-effect explanation.

NONVERBAL FAR-FROM-EQUILIBRIUM CHALLENGES

Information is not just verbal and not just a matter of cognitively appraising a system. As knowledge available to a system about its pattern of relationships, information is also a sense of how the system is organized, structured, and patterned. That is why we can use nonverbal methods to generate far-from-equilibrium conditions in a work group and organization. Such nonverbal methods can include drawings, organizational maps, and human sculptures, all generated by the members of the group.

Such nonverbal methods achieve their power to generate a far-from-equilibrium condition by representing and then challenging systemic patterns in the organization. The nonverbal modality can allow insights, and knowledge available to the system to surface, that might otherwise never see the light of day in an organization that is exclusively preoccupied with verbal and cognitive appraisals of its own functioning. That is, the nonverbal representation may be able to side-step the equilibrium dominance that shows itself in habitually limited ways of problem-solving and decision-making.

Of course, nonverbal creativity practices that use drawings have been around a long time. But as a generator of far-from-equilibrium conditions, nonverbal creativity focuses on the transformative process of self-organization. This is not creativity practice for the sake of better problem-solving or decision-making. Rather, the emphasis is on a nonverbal access to information about the systemic dimension of the organization, that is, tacit knowledge the system contains about its own functioning. Nonverbal means can uncover this tacit knowledge. Let's take a look at how nonverbal systemic representations were used to generate far-from-equilibrium conditions at a community agency.

SYSTEMIC SCULPTING AT "ARBCO"

The "Area Research in Business Collective" ("ARBCO"), mentioned in Chapter 3, is a clearinghouse that provides information about small business loans, free or inexpensive business consulting, fund-raising sources, and government grants for its urban community. "ARBCO" also researches housing, medical care, crime, census data, and population demographics. The director of the program and the two other administrators also hold appointments at the local community college. Fifteen volunteers do most of the agency's work.

Because of their tremendous success, demands for their services quickly exceeded their capacity and both the paid and volunteer staff felt overwhelmed. As a result, the director and her two staff persons felt they needed to rethink their operating structure and make some changes. Two consultants were contracted to conduct an interview-based assessment and lead a retreat and follow-up meetings.

Two major events took place at the retreat: a group sculpture and subgroup mission statements. The group sculpture consisted of each member placing their chairs in relation to the other members' chairs to reflect how they saw their relationships and allegiances to others in the organization. Everyone did this at the same time, generating, of course, pandemonium. Members of the group were encouraged to negotiate their positions if there was a conflict. After the tumult quieted down, they were to hold their positions and observe where they found themselves. Then, each had an opportunity to each talk about why he or she placed his or her chair in those positions. For example, the director was in the middle and she felt she had to do all the work and hold all the expectations. The others wanted to be close to her, which caused a bunching up of chairs near the center.

It is important to notice that this nonverbal sculpture was facilitated before any formal roles were clarified. The latter is a typical OD intervention that generates more clarity about who does what. But, the group sculpture allowed the nonverbal knowledge the system had about its own functioning to manifest and be used by the organization. This nonverbal systemic method generates information (see Chapters 6 and 7). Rather than seeking consensus on roles, the process encourages differences of perception, and thereby, generates information.

In the afternoon, the group had to define the subgroups, determine who would be in each, then break up into the subgroups and establish mission statements for each. Three subgroups eventually formed: one was interested only in researching issues, another was interested in applying research to the real world, the third was interested in educating the community about business opportunities. At the follow-up meeting to the retreat, without the change agents' advocacy, the group decided to form a steering committee to create an organizational mechanism to address the ongoing work of "ARBCO."

FAR-FROM-EQUILIBRIUM CHALLENGES ARE MEANS AS WELL AS OUTCOMES

Finally, it needs to be stressed that because of nonlinearity, far-from-equilibrium challenges are not about butting heads or overpowering resistance. Nor are they a way to use persuasion against resistance, sell the change, disarm the resistance, or to otherwise mobilize an organization to fight it's supposed resistance.

When self-organization occurs, parts of the system are now in greater coordination and communication with each other. This greater coordination is the goal of self-organization and also the way to bring about self-organization. Participative means are not simply the means toward change, they are inherent in the way the system becomes characterized by greater communication and transfer of information. Thus, when self-organization truly takes place, the far-from-equilibrium challenge becomes an inherent aspect of the way the system now goes about its business of staying vitally connected with its environments.

Challenging Federal Metals with "Wicked Questions"

Brenda Zimmerman, a professor at York University and an organizational consultant, provides an example of challenging a work group towards self-organization by using "wicked questions." These wicked questions are the means toward the strategic planning goal, but they are also incorporated into the operation of the company.

Federal Metals is a subsidiary of Fedmet, Inc., which has 67 plants in Canada and throughout the world.[3] Their strategic planning process is unique in the way it links up the purpose of each strategic goal with a wicked question that compares the goal with the current status of the company. As the designers of the strategic planning process put it, a strategic planning document that ends up with foregone conclusions is a farce since these conclusions do not inspire people to achieve anything. Instead, the strategic planning document ends up with goals tied to wicked questions.

For example, the following are two of the strategic plans and accompanying wicked questions for 1990 to 1994:

Goal: Create and maintain an appropriate environment
Wicked questions:
 • Do our body language and our everyday actions reflect what we write?
 • Are we committed to practicing this?
 • If so, what changes does this require in our own style?

Goal: Mobilize and empower front-line people
Wicked question:
 • Are we ready to put responsibility for work on the shoulders of the people who do it?

Asking the wicked question challenges the organization to assimilate its goals in a self-organizing manner. A contrast is established between the goal or purpose in the plan and the actual circumstances. This difference is not downplayed, but is expanded by a constant challenge incorporated into the operation.

This amplification of differences is a far-from-equilibrium condition that primes the pump of self-organization. For example, at one meeting where senior managers were planning strategy, one of the executives picked up his appointment book and said, "Look, we say all this stuff, but I can't find one thing in my book that relates to any of it!"

In this chapter we looked at various features constituting effective far-from-equilibrium challenges, but we still have not gone to the limit of what is possible for generating far-from-equilibrium conditions. That's the job of Chapter 10.

10

THE MAGIC THEATER

All say the Way seems like folly.
But it is great
Because it seems like folly.
Were it not like folly,
It would indeed be petty.
—TAO TE CHING (VERSE 67)

Consider these features of nonlinear systems: orderly patterns emerge out of random events: small events have huge effects; huge efforts have negligible effects; and, mistakes can lead to profound new directions. Indeed, the behavior of nonlinear systems can seem strange, bizarre, and even counterintuitive. But, of course, nonlinearity appears to be counterintuitive only because our intuition has developed in a linear and equilibrium framework. Nonlinear systems, then, require a kind of nonlinear intuition to help us navigate through the strange currents of the nonlinear world.

In an important sense, this nonlinear intuition is nothing new. The best of managers and other change agents always have a bit of "magic" in their approach to implementing organizational change. Indeed, Beer and Walton, in their study of what makes change agents effective, discovered they need decidedly nonlinear skills and awareness.[1] Change agents need to realize that organizations are messy; they need to be able to tolerate ambiguity; they need to be opportunistic; they need to respond flexibly to events as they unfold; and they need to reduce their reliance on normative models and programmed change strategies. In other words, nonlinear change requires nonlinear methods, so self-organization requires an appropriation of disproportionality, unpredictability,

155

complexity, and randomness. Generating far-from-equilibrium conditions, then, is like establishing a *magic theater* where the necessary ingredients of self-organization can be concocted and enacted.

A change agent must take advantage of accidents, crises, and fortuitous events. A change agent needs to apply a bit of the absurd, the strange, and the complex, then find a key role for play, paradox, accidents, and fun. This is particularly the case when the equilibrium conditions in the organization emphasize work, not play; unidirectionality, not paradox; planning, not randomness; and seriousness, rather than fun. All work and no play does not a far-from-equilibrium condition make.

W. Gibb Dyer, Jr. provides many examples of how chance and crises have been significant in transforming corporate cultures.[2] Let's just look at how three types of unexpected events can have this effect. First, there is the unexpected financial crisis; for example, Levi Strauss's European Division suddenly lost $12 million in 1973, which led to a reevaluation of the previously very successful laissez-faire management style in the company. Second, there are new government regulations or new interpretations of those regulations; for example, when the FTC ordered Balfour, the fraternity-ring company, to stop making long-term contracts with customers, they could no longer continue to function in the way they did when they had a 98 percent market share.

Balfour also gives us an example of the third type of unexpected event that can transform a company: the head of the company, L.J. Balfour, died, and subsequently his chief aide was fired. The new president then set out to rid the company of its old paternalism and favoritism.

Events such as these spur change and need to be used to advantage during the process of transformation. Life is an ever-changing and unpredictable process just as self-organization is, so a model of change based on self-organization is better at incorporating the unexpected.

BEYOND PLANNING AND PREDICTION

Accidents, unplanned events, coincidence, crises—all of these are a prevalent and crucial occurrence in organizational change efforts, yet the traditional approach has no place for them. For example, the traditional OD model of change puts a high premium on planning, deliberation, and prediction in order to keep the unplanned and accidental to a bare minimum. Zeira and Avedisian took this mania for planning and prediction to an extreme with a planning tool that supposedly can predict the success or failure of an organizational change intervention.[3] Supposedly, if their diagnostic tool ascertains that the necessary organizational factors are present, then the change can proceed successfully; if not, the various conditions that are lacking have to be remedied, or the change effort should be scrapped.

Consider the theoretical basis of this kind of planning tool: it supposedly works by capturing an instantaneous picture of the organization that is then used as a basis for projecting into the future. The hope is that if this is an accurate picture of the initial conditions of the system, and the processes affecting system change are known, then the desired outcome is predictable before the actual intervention begins. These kinds of tools have led organization development to be called the planned change approach.

As nonlinear systems evolve under the influence of far-from-equilibrium conditions, however, no planning approach can predict what will transpire, and no shortcut can tell the future; you just have to watch the system evolve. Chance alone decides which of the possible alternative configurations will be realized during self-organization.[4] When a far-from-equilibrium condition challenges a nonlinear system to find a more effective manner of functioning, the system scans its situation, perhaps makes a few unsuccessful attempts, and finally amplifies a particular, random departure from equilibrium that takes over the system. The ensuing history of the system follows from this critical chance event. The far-from-equilibrium condition enables the appropriation of the unexpected, not the planned. Let's look at an example of how the unexpected took precedence over the planned.

UNPLANNED CONSEQUENCES AT "MICHIGAN MOTORS"

According to management theorist F. Westley, top management at "Michigan Motors" decided to redesign one of its plants in order to improve the quality of the cars.[5] The ensuing organizational change project attempted to establish a participative and integrative structure as a collateral arrangement to the current hierarchy. This intervention, however, did not meet with a great deal of success initially. Activities in the collateral structure were just not as effective as the already existing management chain of command! As might be expected, they attributed the failure to resistance arising from the deeply rooted corporate culture.

Yet, spontaneous effects did occur that were not anticipated by the planned change intervention. Certain employees experienced a conversion to a different view of their role in the organization. As one of these converts put it:

> What happened was that the operating committee just quit following things up and the people themselves didn't know how to interpret the data, how to find out the data, how to prioritize things in terms of the data they had. We had, in fact, to retrain people about what things meant.[6]

This retraining about the meaning of basic operating practices led to a spontaneous and infectious questioning of how they should organize workers most effectively to produce a quality car. And, this questioning process went on to have profound repercussions on how managers understood their managerial roles, and how subordinates viewed managerial influence.

It was these converts, not the original consultants, who became the spontaneous, internal change agents and facilitated a more participative environment. So, perhaps the intervention at this automobile plant was not such a failure after all. The unrehearsed reformulation of roles that took place was actually more crucial to the long-run transformation needed by the plant.

FROM NOISE TO SERENDIPITY

It is not only the unplanned that plays a critical role in the process of self-organizing transformation, it is also the *unwanted*. In systems talk, this unwanted element is usually called *noise* to distinguish it from the wanted *signal* in a transmitting device. For example, when you tune a radio to find a station, you try to move away from the static or *noise* and move towards a clear signal. From the perspective of a preset station, this noise is an unwanted intrusion. Thinking from the perspective of a preset station is an equilibrium way of thinking that is analogous to the equilibrium-maintaining function of a thermostat set to a predetermined comfort range. In other words, noise is only noise when the prearranged equilibrium conditions demarcate it as noise. It is only from this equilibrium perspective that noise is considered an unwanted intrusion to be eliminated.

Chapter 3 described the equilibrium condition of the Benard liquid as like a lake that only appears calm on its surface, while underneath are many random currents. Similarly, in an organization where self-fulfilling prophecies maintain equilibrium, random events take place that are not allowed to influence the operation of the working unit. These random events are the noise the equilibrium process seeks to eliminate.

Controlling random events by eliminating discrepancies from equilibrium is supposed to be a key management function. This is based on a tenet of traditional management theory that unexpected, random events, that is, organizational noise, are destructive to the proper functioning of the unit.

Organizational noise can be any out-of-the-norm event including:[7]

- Differences between the way a machine should operate and the way it actually does, for example, an unexpected breakdown

- Variation in production or service parameters, such as variations in temperature in a production process where only average temperatures are used to adjust the process

- Fluctuations in attendance or absentee rates, not just at work but at meetings, training programs, etc.

- Perturbations in order rates, customer complaints, or service calls that need to be made

- Workers who remain at their stations after work to play around with their projects in different ways

- Managers trying new methods right after attending a seminar

- Temporary reorganizations to put together a new piece of equipment or to fill in when a member is absent

- Accidents or "mistakes" of any kind

- Temporary crises of any kind

- Illnesses of members of a work group

What is common to these examples of organizational *noise* is that they are unexpected, diverse phenomena occurring in or around the organization that are usually disregarded under normal functioning.

Self-organization, however, has revealed that under a far-from-equilibrium condition, noise may assume a critical role in the evolution of the system if it is amplified instead of eliminated. The new pattern can't be predicted, however, nor can it be established ahead of time which noise will have a transformative effect. Of course, that's been the problem—knowing what to do with noise, when it doesn't fit into the neat little equilibrium and control package of traditional management philosophy.

Recognizing and incorporating the random element of noise, and the concomitant new patterns that emerge, can be a creative development for an organizational system. The organization can use the chance or noisy event to explore or test different system configurations. The noise may represent an evolutionary response of the social system to changes in the environment. The fluctuations of systems, the noisy events, rather than the norm-seeking, average behavior may be crucial for a system to learn about the world around it.[8] For example, dogs who go off the beaten track find things to eat more frequently than dogs who roam only in the same old ruts. Cogent evidence shows that a permanent and rigid structure in a system that interacts with an unpredictable environment is not as good a strategy as developing temporary structures that are suitable for any occasion that may arise.[9]

TAKING ADVANTAGE OF SERENDIPITY

Not all noise is good noise. Obviously, some measure of controlling noise is necessary. After all, who wants to listen to static rather a clear radio station? The problem in controlling noise, however, is what noise do we eliminate and what noise do we amplify? A helpful guideline for managing organizational change in this context is to make creative use of serendipitous noise. Serendipity is the key, but what exactly is this elusive phenomenon?

James Austin indicated that many scientific discoveries were the result of the scientist taking advantage of a chance occurrence, that is, *serendipity*.[10] A classic example is how Alexander Fleming discovered penicillin by noticing the effect of a mold that fell accidentally onto a culture dish. It wasn't merely the accident, though, it was also Fleming's preparedness to take advantage of the accident by fusing together five previously unrelated elements:

- I see that a mold has fallen by accident into my culture dish.

- The staphylococcal colonies residing near it failed to grow.

- Therefore, the mold must have secreted something that killed the bacteria.

- This reminds me of a similar experience I had once before.

- Maybe, this new "something" from the mold could be used to kill staphylococci that cause human infections.

Austin is not implying that a scientist must wait around for luck to spring forth. Instead, a scientist can only take advantage of chance if she or he is prepared. This requires cultivating a *creative* approach. For Austin, the creative researcher "...must remain ready to change tactics (always), strategy (many times), and policy (less commonly, but whenever the situation warrants)...much of the novelty in creativity is decided only when you are bold enough to thrust at chance."[11] As Louis Pasteur once said, "Chance favors the prepared mind."

Serendipity is the key. The creative spirit lunges at the serendipitous chance event, the fluctuation, the accident, the fortuitousness circumstance, the mutation prompted by a difficult and challenging situation. Again, in Austin's words, "...we have learned since Gregor Mendel's day how it happens that a rare but helpful mutation enables a bean plant to survive unusually difficult extremes of temperature. But, until we have exposed the plant to such extremes, the potential effect of its mutation lies hidden, dormant."[12]

It is no different for the change agent who facilitates organizational change. Organizational change also is often a matter of taking advantage of serendipity. For example, Dyer found that, more often than not, organizational change was not so much the result of planning, but was instead precipitated by *unanticipated* financial shifts, crises, illnesses, and even the death of leaders. "Serendipity and historical accidents played critical roles, and while it may be possible to anticipate such occurrences, manager's abilities to control these events are negligible."[13] Dyer suggests that to initiate cultural change, the key leaders in an organization must have a sense of *timing* that enables them to seize the opportunity for change when it arises. It is this timing that links organizational noise to the intended changes.

A successful change agent needs to encourage creative organizational responses, not by anticipating the unpredictable, but by taking advantage of the unpredictable when it inevitably occurs. This is not to suggest that planning has no use. Every organizational intervention needs a design but the design is simply a place to get started, not a hard and fast procrustean bed.

In fact, the ability to predict and control a future organizational configuration may actually be an obstacle to organizational creativity since it is of the very nature of creative processes that they bring into play a novel element. Obviously, this novel element cannot emerge if a change strategy is based too closely on a linear prediction that supposedly anticipates what will happen and what will be significant. But, an organizational system that functions in a nonlinear and far-from-equilibrium fashion evolves in a creative way that is not predictable ahead of time.[14]

During self-organization new patterns emerge as the system organizes. These new patterns signify creative emergence since the system has found an alternative way of patterning itself to accomplish its purpose of exchange with the environment. But this means that the essence of self-organization is a creative process; creative in the sense that the system explores and selects alternative ways of being patterned. Let's see an example of how this serendipity plays itself out in surprising ways during the process of organizational change.

Serendipity at "The Midwest Institute"

We saw in Chapter 8 that during the implementation of a TQM program at "The Midwest Institute," the averaging of survey results led to a degeneration of information. During this same organizational change effort, an unexpected event played a key role in unfolding change that illustrates the serendipitous use of organizational noise.

The TQM project was being installed in a department of the "Institute" that consisted of 40 professionals and 30 support staff. One of the focus areas of the project was management style. Recently, the department had received additional work from the "Institute" without an accompanying increase in staff. The extra work strained the current operation and the department director was seemingly helpless in addressing the issue. Also, the management style of the department head clashed with the TQM recommendations.

As a result, many of the questions in the initial survey concerned the director's managerial practices, for example, the appropriateness of his behavior in meetings. Accompanying the survey were the customary interviews with department members as well as some of the department's clients in other areas of the institute.

As it turned out, both the survey and assessment results were not flattering to either the department director or his assistant. These unflattering results left the consultants who were in charge of the project in a quandary: How could they present the findings without creating defensiveness that would block the assimilation of the information? They decided to coach each other by role playing how to present the data in a nonthreatening way, and coaching the steering committee before it received the survey data. In addition, they chose to not present any comments that were not mentioned by at least two different members of the department.

Now, unbeknownst to the consultants, the department was on a institutionally-based, five-year rotation for an intensive performance review conducted by senior management. One week before the consultants were to deliver the assessment results to the steering committee and the department director, the department head received a very blunt five-year review. The review pinpointed the director's management style and strongly suggested improvements.

The consultants knew nothing of this harsh review, however. But, serendipitously, when the steering committee finally met and the department director heard the negative feedback, he was already primed by his previous review to be more responsive to the information. The serendipitous mix of the review with the TQM survey results created a nonlinear, amplifying interaction that made the feedback more powerful to effectuate change. The department received a double whammy of information. In fact, the consultant who spearheaded the change effort credited this serendipitous two-pronged confrontation with feedback as a major factor that led to change in the department.

FIND THE LEANING TOWER AND PUSH IT OVER

Being on the lookout for serendipity is not the only way a consultant can foster the utilization of organizational noise. Sometimes the change agent has to go right for the noise and amplify it to interrupt the equilibrium processes in the system. In Chapter 7 we remarked on how family therapists have evolved many techniques for getting families beyond dysfunctional patterns. Many of these techniques focus on upsetting the equilibrium-seeking tendency of the family that keep it stuck in old, dysfunctional patterns. For example, difference questioning can amplify, not disregard, the differences in perception and feeling between the different members. The effect of these differences demolishes the myth of a monolithic, conforming picture of the family. But these methods of equilibrium-busting are not limited to difference questioning.

One of the master practitioners of equilibrium-busting in families is Carl Whitaker, famous for his use of the *absurd* in dislodging the dominance of equilibrium.[15] Whitaker first tries to discover those noisy elements in the family process that point to already existing underlying departures from equilibrium. He calls these elements in the family "The Leaning Tower," for they lean away from the norm. Whitaker uses methods of absurdity to push over these leaning towers. He explained the goal of his method was, "...to increase the complexity of the situation...to induce chaos and craziness rather than to restore order...My tactic has become a tongue-in-cheek put-on, an induced chaos now called positive feedback—that is, we augment the pathology until the symptoms self-destruct."

Whitaker offers the following examples to illustrate his use of absurd methods to push over the leaning tower:

- Give the top of an old coffee percolator to a family member on the way out of a session without an explanation.

- Give a patient, who supposedly has a "weak ego boundary," a large sheet of blank paper with an X marked on it to "use as ego boundary as needed."

- Leave the session unannounced and return in five minutes saying, "My foot itched."

- Write a letter during the session to a co-therapist entitled, "Why this family won't make it" and offer it to any member who questions the writing behavior.

These seemingly ridiculous interventions are calculated to shock, amaze, enchant, and confuse in order to break old patterns of thought and behavior. Whitaker cautions that such absurd maneuvers must be done in a context of loving care and safety. This is another way of talking about the need for firm and safe boundaries as we discussed in Chapter 7.

In Whitaker's absurd ploys, we find a use of exaggeration, of caricature, of unexpected actions. Objects out-of-the-blue are used to jar the equilibrium. At the bottom of this absurdity is a reliance on the change agent's nonlinear intuition. This kind of nonlinear intuition, of course, is not amenable to planning, but it can be learned through practice.

To be sure, organizations are different from families, and organizational change agents are not expected to practice family therapy on work groups. There is a carryover, however, in terms of the need to dislodge the dominance of equilibrium in order to allow the system to change. The powerful attraction of equilibrium-seeking in the groups, whether familial or organizational, calls for equally powerful methods to generate far-from-equilibrium conditions, so that the innate potential for growth inherent in the system can be released. In organizational change, absurdity can be employed by using theatrical or dramatic gestures, by exaggerating current practices or beliefs, and doing things that appear to be just plain silly.

Managerial Magic Makes Use of Absurdity

In their book *Managerial Magic*,[16] Richard Nodell and Eric Wolff offer several other examples of using absurdity, paradox, and playfulness in organizational change interventions.

Taking advantage of random associations. When bogged down in a meeting, the manager or change agent can make a game out of associating the current situation with completely irrelevant experiences or objects. For example, "This job is like a cement mixer." "This project is like a bathtub." Then let the group come up with their own interpretations and associations with these metaphors. These metaphoric excursions certainly get the group off the equilibrium dime.

Communicating paradoxical messages. Give messages that contain contradictory sides. For example, during a meeting with a Human Resources Department that was struggling to formulate a new direction, the consultants felt the group was avoiding the confusion and bewilderment that come with real creative work. As feedback to the group, one of the consultants said, one of us thinks you have worked real hard and deserve to rest tonight, the other thinks you haven't accomplished a thing and should stay up all night to catch up.

This sort of paradox can shock a group into the requisite confusion for creative work. After all if the group is not confused, they are still happy with the way they have been doing things. Then, what is the fuel for self-organization?

Using anything that happens. Whatever takes place in a group, such as accidents and unplanned events, can be used to generate a far-from-equilibrium condition. For example, in an intervention with a work group that was experiencing a great deal of hopelessness in creating a change, whenever a strategy for dealing with their conflict emerged, someone would inevitably blurt out, "It will never work." The group would go along with this hopeless attitude.

After lunch one day, at a meeting of the work group and the change agents, one of the members looked sick and ran out of the room. Looking better when he returned, he exclaimed that he had eaten too much brisket for lunch. From then on, whenever one of the group asserted a hopeless attitude, the consultant would ask the group if they wanted some brisket!

PLAYING AROUND WITH CHANGE

A crucial ingredient in the self-confirming cycle of a self-fulfilling prophecy is the inherent sense of being right. Because the outcomes resulting from the actions (determined, in turn, by the expectations) are self-confirming, they contain a sense of their own righteousness, that is, they justify themselves. Consequently, the members of the group caught up in the self-fulfilling prophecy take these beliefs, actions, and results very seriously. This seriousness is one of the ways the group continues to buy into the original premise underneath the self-fulfilling prophecy.

If seriousness maintains equilibrium then one remedy for equilibrium is the opposite of seriousness—that is, *play*. Play, not hard work, can bring about deeper transformation.

Therefore, I heartily recommend that to generate deeply rooted organizational change, we need to encourage a spirit of play. Below is just one suggestion of how play can be an important method for changing an organization. The possibilities, of course, are endless.

PLAYING WITH STRANGE ATTRACTORS

Nan Kilkeary, an organizational consultant and author of the book *The Good Communicator*,[17] offers a way for organizations to play with the notion of attractors, a phenomenon of nonlinear systems that we discussed in Chapters 2 through 5. Remember that nonlinear systems under far-from-equilibrium conditions evolve through different phases; each phase is ruled by an attractor. The attractor represents the systemic pattern or context that determines the allowable behavior of the system when it is in that particular attractor regime.

A strange attractor is the weirdly shaped pattern of the phase of a nonlinear system when it evolves into a state of chaos. This chaotic state differs from the traditional meaning of *chaos* as totally random activity. The modern meaning of chaos shows it to be a very complexly ordered pattern that only appears to be random, but is actually evidenced by a strange, new kind of order. Computer-generated diagrams of this strange attractor reveal a bizarre mixture of convergence and divergence.

The concept of an attractor is intimately linked with the growth potential of a nonlinear system under far-from-equilibrium conditions. It, therefore, can be a powerful metaphoric tool to unleash that growth potential. Here, a work unit or organization is asked to nonverbally represent the attractors that drive their current situation as well as possible attractors that are pulling them into future developments. These nonverbal techniques could include the type of group sculpture that "ARBCO" created (see Chapter 9). It could include drawings or paintings done by individual or by teams, in which each person adds their own unique flourish.

The point is not that these nonverbal representations are accurate mathematical renditions of the actual attractors of the system. Instead, these metaphoric attractors bring about an increase of knowledge available to the system about both its present functioning and possible future trajectories.

Strange Attractors at "Great Lakes Consortium"

The Communications Department at "Great Lakes Consortium," a huge wood products firm, was severely downsized over the past year, along with the rest of the company. The department worked with an external consultant to try and accomplish two interrelated goals: to build a more cohesive team and to develop a long-term mission that would have a significant impact on the whole company.

At one team-building and planning meeting, the consultant introduced certain ideas taken from nonlinear and far-from-equilibrium research. The idea of attractors, specifically the idea of a strange attractor from chaos theory, was highlighted. The consultant introduced the idea of a strange attractor and asked the group to think about their mission in these terms: what was the department's strange attractor, or, what was the pattern that drove their department as a system within the large system of the entire company?

In other words, the consultant was challenging the department to think about their mission as what ultimately attracted the department members. The consultant's strategy in introducing the idea of their strange attractor, was not to make a point about the mathematical relevance of the strange attractor to the department's functioning. Instead, the consultant used the metaphoric power of the concept of the strange attractor to facilitate the group in thinking along new lines as it developed its mission.

The group was given the task of depicting their mission or strange attractor as a drawing. Each member was to draw their version of how

they saw other members, as well as the group as a whole. These drawings made them feel more in touch with their own aspirations, as well as their roles in the bigger picture. They felt revitalized and clearer about what they needed to do in order to accomplish their mission.

The drawing of the strange attractor, then, had a metaphoric power to release creativity in a group that had been seriously compromised during the tumultuous time of downsizing. Moreover, the idea of an attractor, with its connotations of being that toward which the group was being attracted, helped refocus the group on the future with its unbounded creative possibilities, instead of the equilibrium-bound past.

EPILOGUE

When we lose our balance, we die,
but at the same time we also develop ourselves, we grow...
—SHUNRYU SUZUKI ROSHI

The only thing we can say with much certainty anymore is that nothing much is certain. Change, flux, even turbulence have become the name of the game. Businesses and institutions, of course, have always needed to change in order to adapt to the shifting circumstances of changing markets, technological innovations, unforeseen competition, governmental regulations, war, famine, epidemics, and so on. But in our age the pace of change has accelerated to a fever pitch. Indeed, what company or institution is not right now involved in a life and death struggle to survive in a constantly shifting, tumultuous environment?

This struggle to the death is not confined to our organizations. I remember being stunned when in my high school physics class I first heard about the "heat death" of the universe, the depressing idea that the universe would eventually deteriorate into a formless and random incoherence. This was the accepted interpretation of the famous law of entropy or the inevitable tendency of any system toward dissolution and disorder. All systems, including the universe as a whole, would show a continual break-up of order, complexity, pattern, and organization. This final disorder was characterized as a condition of equilibtrium or a state of lowest energy, order, and coherent pattern. Ultimately entropy and equilibrium would assert their dominance.

One of the astounding findings of current research in theoretical physics, however, has been that systems can show an opposite tendency: They have the potential of evolving into states of greater organization, complexity, and order. That is what self-organization is all about—the evolution of nonlinear systems into more complex patterns when they are in far-from-equilibrium conditions. That is why self-organization as a model for organizational change is relevant as our businesses and institutions face so much unprecedented tumult.

The implications of self-organization for the supposed "heat death" fate of the universe are currently being debated by scientists and phlosophers. On a more practical level, however, the good news is we do not need to characterize systems, including our businesses and institutions, as being dominated by a tendency toward equilibrium or resistance to change. Instead, the phenomenon of self-organization affirms that our organizations can be attracted to states of more coherence, more complex order, and more effective functioning. Organizational transformation, then, is about setting up the appropriate conditions whereby this attraction to more effective functioning can take place.

The following list summarizes the essential features of how self-organization can be applied to organizational transformation:

- Businesses and institutions are nonlinear systems

- Nonlinear systems have several crucial properties including their innate capacity for self-organization

- Self-organization represents a system's affinity for evolving into modes of functioning exhibiting more complex and coherent patterns

- Self-organization takes place when a nonlinear system is placed under far-from-equilibirum conditions

- Resistance to change is only a temporary phenomenon, equivalent to the organization's or work unit's attraction to a state of equilibrium

- The state of equilibrium is maintained by self-fulfilling prophecies operating in an organization or work unit

- Far-from-equilibrium conditions interrupt the state of equilibrium by releasing the nonlinearity inherent in self-fulfilling prophecies

- A key to far-from-equilibirum conditions is that they increase the information available to a system concerning its own functioning

- For far-from-equilibrium conditions to lead to self-organizing transformation there must be firm but permeable boundaries in the work group or organization
- The following methods can generate far-from-equilibrium conditions prompting self-organization:
  - difference questioning
  - cultural difference questioning
  - purpose contrasting
  - challenging assumptions creatively
  - experimenting with departures from equilibrium
  - nonverbally representing the organization
  - recognizing and amplifying serendipity
  - using absurdity to take advantage of organizational noise

NOTES

CHAPTER 1

1. Ilya Prigogine and Isabelle Stengers, *Order Out of Chaos: Man's New Dialogue with Nature* (New York: Bantam, 1984).

2. Under this term "nonlinear systems theory" can be included the following areas of research: far-from-equilibrium thermodynamics; chaos theory; nonlinear dynamical systems theory; complex adaptive systems theory; anti-chaos theory; the theory of organized self-criticality; cellular automata; and other approaches to the phenomenon of self-organization. See the following works:

   R. Abraham and C. Shaw, *Dynamics: The Geometry of Behavior, Part Two: Chaotic Behavior* (Santa Cruz, Calif.: Aerial Press, 1984).

   S. Kauffman, *The Origins of Order: Self-Organization and Selection in Evolution* (New York: Oxford Univ. Press, 1993).

   R. Lewin, *Complexity: Life at the Edge of Chaos* (New York: Macmillan, 1992).

   G. Nicolis and I. Prigogine, *Exploring Complexity* (New York: W.H. Freeman & Co., 1989).

   M. Waldrop, Complexity: *The Emerging Science at the Edge of Order and Chaos* (New York: Simon & Schuster, 1992).

3. Traditionally, scientists focused on linear and avoided nonlinear equations. For example, J. Doyne Farmer recounts how physics textbooks relegated nonlinearity to the back of the book, and even there reduced it to a set of linear approximations (cited in James Gleick, *Chaos: Making a New Science* [New York: Viking, 1987], pp. 250, 251). The recent advent of computers and computer-aided graphics, though, has created a renewed interest in nonlinear mathematics.

   Even the term "nonlinearity" is not of much help since it is defined negatively: not being linear. The mathematician Ian Stewart has pointed out that defining nonlinearity as the negation of linearity is akin to calling all animals besides elephants non-pachyderms! (Stewart, *Does God Play Dice: The*

Mathematics of Chaos [London: Basil Blackwell, 1989], p. 84.) Hopefully, since we are only at the beginning of the advent of the age of nonlinearity, better terms will surely be forthcoming.

4. See the model of "quasi-stationary equilibrium levels" in Kurt Lewin, *Field Theory in Social Science* (New York: Harper & Row, 1951).

5. See the discussion on equilibrium models in social science in Cynthia Russett, *The Concept of Equilibrium in American Social Thought* (New Haven: Yale Univ. Press, 1966). Equilibrium models in psychology are discussed in Sophie Haroutunian, *Equilibrium in the Balance: A Study of Psychological Explanation* (New York: Springer-Verlag, 1983); and Jeffrey Goldstein, "Unbalancing Psychoanalytic Thought: Beyond Freud's Equilibrium Model," in R. Robertson, ed., *Proceedings of The Society for Chaos Theory in Psychology* (Forthcoming, 1994).

6. For a discussion on the problems with the concepts of equilibrium and its cousin concept, homeostasis, see Anthony Wilden, *System and Structure* (London: Tavistock, 1980)

7. Rather than a "Balance of Nature," contemporary ecologists follow the physics of self-organization and speak of a balance between order and chaos at the "edge of chaos." The edge of "chaos" is a realm in the evolution of a dynamical system which is characterized neither by a rigid structure nor by mere chaotic anarchy, but instead is a place that allows for the optimization of novelty and innovation; see Lewin, *Complexity*, op. cit. In this way, the "edge of chaos" allows a system to maintain its "autopoietic" integrity, i.e., its robustness in the face of a constantly changing environment; see H. Maturana and F. Varela, *Autopoiesis and Cognition: The Realization of the Living* (Dordrecht, Holland: D. Reidel Publishing Co., 1980).

CHAPTER 2

1. Cited in John Bigelow, "A Catastrophe Model of Organizational Change," *Behavioral Science* 27: 26-42, 1982.

2. Feedback is typically separated into two types: positive and negative (please note that these terms are not value judgments about the feedback). Negative feedback refers to a nonlinear inhibition of a quantity. An example is a self-regulation process such as found in a thermostat. When the temperature in a room exceeds the pre-set top limit, say 70 degrees, the thermometer inside the thermostat "notices" this and sends a message to either turn off the heat (in winter) or turn on the air conditioning (in summer). This action will then decrease the temperature. There is a negative feedback loop between the thermostat and the room air temperature.

Nonlinear, negative feedback mechanisms are at work in our bodies as they maintain a fairly constant temperature of 98.6 degrees. This negative feedback has been called homeostasis since an equilibrium region (rest or stasis) is maintained. It is a process of self-regulation because the system is regulated by some internal mechanism like a thermostat to stay within a certain equilibrium range of some value.

On the other hand, positive feedback occurs when, instead of a dampening effect, there is an amplification—for example, the screech produced by a microphone placed too close to a speaker.

The system dynamics school of organizational research, founded by Jay Forrester at MIT, relies heavily on the notions of positive and negative feedback in its loop diagrams of organizational functioning. Thus areas of growth and expansion are positive feedback loops, whereas areas of limitations or self-regulating processes are negative feedback loops. Such diagrams help in intimating how various changes will affect the system as well as in understanding what seem to be counterintuitive behaviors in a system when changes are made.

3. For an explanation of the mathematics behind predictability, see Ivar Ekeland, *Mathematics and the Unexpected* (Chicago: Univ. of Chicago Press, 1988).

4. Kurt Lewin, *Field Theory in Social Science* (New York: Harper & Row, 1951).

5. For a recounting of Lorenz's discovery see the eminently readable, James Gleick, *Chaos: Making a New Science* (New York: Viking, 1987).

6. Ian Stewart, *Does God Play Dice: The Mathematics of Chaos* (London: Basil Blackwell, 1989), p. 83.

7. For a somewhat sophisticated discussion of how nonlinear phenomena were treated by linear approximations see Bruce West, *An Essay on the Importance of Being Nonlinear* (Berlin: Springer-Verlag, 1985).

8. See, for example, the systems approach of Peter M. Senge, *The Fifth Discipline: The Art and Practice of the Learning Organization* (New York: Doubleday Currency, 1990).

CHAPTER 3

1. The discussion on self-organization in this chapter has been greatly influenced by the explanation of this process offered by Gregoire Nicolis in his article, "Physics of Far-from-equilibrium Systems and Self-organization," in

The New Physics, ed. Paul Davies (Cambridge: Cambridge Univ. Press, 1989). See also Gregoire Nicolis and Ilya Prigogine, Exploring Complexity: An Introduction (New York: W.H. Freeman & Co., 1989).

2. What happened at Semco is recounted by its owner/chief executive Ricardo Semler in his article, "Managing Without Managers," Harvard Business Review, September/October 1989, pp. 76-84.

3. For an example of the importance of information flow in self-organization, see the work of Chris Langton in bringing about self-organization in cellular automata by manipulating the amount of information flow. Langton's work is recounted in Steven Levy's Artificial Life: A Report from the Frontier Where Computers Meet Biology (New York: Vintage Books, 1992).

4. Ikujiro Nonaka, "Creating Organizational Order out of Chaos: Self-renewal in Japanese Firms," California Management Review 30(3): 57-73 (1988).

5. For a discussion of the necessary conditions for self-organization in various liquids, see P. Berge, I. Pomeau, and C. Vidal, Order within Chaos: Towards a Deterministic Approach to Turbulence (New York: John Wiley & Sons, 1984).

6. See the popular account of "chemical clocks" by Malcolm Browne titled, "Chemists' New Tools: Molecular See-Saws," New York Times, April 28, 1992, p. C1.2

7. An example of unbounded positive feedback is the instability associated with amplification of deviations from equilibrium as an airplane flies. Imagine a plane trying to maintain stability in the face of air turbulence. The pilot tries to keep this kind of instability in the plane's motion to a bare minimum. That is, the pilot tries to keep tremors on the wings from amplifying into wide wobbles that might eventually lead to the pilot losing control of the plane. This kind of amplification away from equilibrium does not signify the emergence of any kind of useful ordered structure as is found in self-organization, since there is no firm, boundaried region that could harness the amplifications in a constructive direction.

8. There is an important way that information is gained in nonlinear systems such as those characterized as "chaotic." For a very technical analysis of this phenomenon, see Robert Shaw's article, "Strange Attractors, Chaotic Behavior, and Information Flow," Zeitschrift for Naturforschung, 36a, 1981, pp. 80-112. For a less technical account of Shaw's work, see Abraham and Shaw (1984), cited in Chapter 1, note 2.

9. See Jeffrey Goldstein's article, "Beyond Planning and Prediction: Bringing back Action Research of O.D.," Organization Development Journal 10(2): 1-8 (Summer, 1992).

CHAPTER 4

1. Jeffrey Goldstein, "A Far-From-Equilibrium approach to Resistance to Change," *Organizational Dynamics* 17 (2): 16-22 (1988).

2. See, e.g., Roy Schafer, *A New Language for Psychoanalysis* (New Haven: Yale Univ. Press, 1976); and Yvonne Dolan, *A Path with a Heart: Ericksonian Utilization with Resistant and Chronic Clients* (New York: Brunner/Mazel, 1985).

3. This example is taken from Peter Reynolds, "Imposing a Corporate Culture," *Psychology Today* 21(3): 32-38 (1987).

   Corporate culture is the organizational counterpart to an individual's belief system. It is a way of talking about the underlying relation between the organization's dominant norms of behavior, sense of mission, and managerial styles. Corporate culture is thought to act as a hidden resistance not immediately obvious like organizational structure, work team composition, productivity goals, or management policies. From its position under the surface of the organization, culture can be like a fifth column superseding the conscious, surface policies and, thus getting in the way of change interventions.

4. See, e.g., the criticism of equilibrium/homeostatic models of social systems in Cynthia Russet, *The Concept of Equilibrium in American Social Thought* (New Haven: Yale Univ. Press, 1966); and Anthony Wilden, System and Structure (London: Tavistock, 1980).

CHAPTER 5

1. Michael Corey, "Delta Airlines' Problems as a Function of a Self-fulfilling Prophecy," *Psychology: A Journal of Human Behavior* 25 (2): 59-64. The sociologist Robert King Merton was the first social scientist to discuss the self-fulfilling prophecy. The structure and examples of the SFP in the rest of the chapter follow from his early. See a discussion of Merton's insights in George Richardson, *The Feedback Concept in American Social Science, with Implications for System Dynamics.* System Dynamic Group Paper #D-3417, presented at International System Dynamics Conference, July, 1983).

2. The SFP is the organizational analogue to what happens during autocatalysis in chemical reactions, a process necessary for self-organization in so-called chemical clocks. In a chemical clock, there is a process of self-organization characterized by an amazing periodic rhythm of clock-like changes in color and pattern.

In autocatalysis a chemical compound nonlinearly catalyzes itself. This means the presence of a particular compound in a chemical reaction enhances the rate of its own production. The more there is of the compound, the faster it is produced, and the faster it is produced, the more there is of it, and so on in an accelerating pace.

Yet, a curious thing about autocatalysis is that although it is clearly a nonlinear process, this nonlinearity is masked when the chemical reaction is at equilibrium conditions. This is similar to how equilibrium conditions mask the inherent nonlinearity of the Benard liquid as mentioned in Chapter 3. Thus, autocatalysis becomes a key ingredient in the chemical system's self-organization only when the chemical reaction is in a far-from-equilibrium condition.

For more on chemical clocks, see Malcolm W. Browne, "Chemists' New Tools: Molecular See-Saws," *New York Times,* April 28, 1992, pp. C1 and C7.

3. See, for example, the work of Dov Eden and Richard Field on the role of self-fulfilling expectations in leadership (Dov Eden, "Self-fulfilling Prophecy as a Management Tool: Harnessing Pygmalion," *Academy of Management Review* 9 [1]: 64-73 [1984]; and Richard Field, "The Self-fulfilling Prophecy Leader: Achieving the Metharme Effect," *Journal of Management Studies* 26 [2]: 153-175 [March 1989]).

4. This example is the subject of the social-scientific investigation of this group as recounted in Leon Festinger, Henry Riecken, and Stanley Schachter, *When Prophecy Fails* (New York: Harper & Row, 1956).

5. The typewriter example is taken from Gareth Morgan, *Images of Organization* (Beverly Hills: Sage, 1986).

6. The story about what transpired at Johnsonville Foods is recounted by its CEO, Ralph Stayer, in his article "How I Learned to Let My Workers Lead," *Harvard Business Review,* November/December 1990, pp. 66-83.

7. R. Rosenthal and L. Jacobson, *Pygmalion in the Classroom* (New York: Holt, 1968).

8. Mentioned in Edgar Peters, *Chaos and Order in the Capital Markets* (New York: John Wiley & Sons, 1991). Peters even found that the time length and degree of the nonlinearity of these trends is connected to the kind of industry. For example, stocks in high-tech companies with high levels of innovation have stronger trends with shorter cycles than stable, uninnovative organizations such as utility companies.

9. W. Brian Arthur, "Positive Feedbacks in the Economy," *Scientific American,* February 1990, pp. 92-99.

10. Mark Snyder and William Swann, "Behavioral Confirmation in Social Interaction: From Social Perception to Social Reality," *Journal of Experimental Social Psychology* 14 (2): 148-162 (March 1978).

11. On placebo research, see Leonard White, Bernard Tursky, and Gary Schwartz, eds., *Placebo: Theory, Research, and Mechanisms* (New York: Guilford Press, 1985).

12. This story is told in Bruno Klopfer, "Psychological Variables in Human Cancer," *Journal of Projective Techniques* 21: 331-340 (1957).

13. Gareth Morgan, *Images of Organization*, note 5 above.

14. Ian Mitroff and Richard Mason, *Challenging Strategic Planning Assumptions: Theory, Cases, and Techniques* (New York: John Wiley & Sons, 1981).

15. Brenda Zimmerman explores what happens to strategy in the context of far-from-equilibrium conditions in her article, "The Inherent Drive Towards Chaos," in *Implementing Strategic Processes: Change, Learning, and Cooperation*, ed. P. Lorange, B. Chakravarty, A. Van de Ven, and J. Roos (London: Basil Blackwell, 1992).

CHAPTER 6

1. The use of families to illustrate the role of information in social systems is strongly indebted to the Milan School of Systemic Family Therapy as found in Luigi Boscolo, Gianfranco Cecchin, Lynn Hoffman, and Peggy Penn, *Milan Systemic Family Therapy* (New York: Basic Books, 1987).

2. Jeremy Campbell, *Grammatical Man: Information, Entropy, Language, and Life* (New York: Simon & Schuster, 1982).

CHAPTER 7

1. H. Atlan, "On a Formal Definition of Organization," *The Journal of Theoretical Biology* 45: 295-304 (1974).

2. Larry Hirschhorn and Thomas Gilmore, "The New Boundaries of the 'Boundaryless Organization,'" *Harvard Business Review*, May/June 1992, pp. 104-115.

3. This example is taken from Jeffrey Goldstein, "The Unconscious Life of Organizations: Anxiety, Authority, and Boundaries—An Interview with Larry Hirschhorn," *Organization Development Journal* 10 (4): 15-22 (Winter 1992).

4. Certainly, there will be instances in which there may be disagreement as to what counts and does not count as a system. Being a system is a relative thing, in the same way that there may be more of a connection between the members in one family than in another. Nevertheless, there will be a way to distinguish a system from nonsystems since the system defines a bounded area where this inner influence is evident, in contrast to what is outside the system.

5. Gareth Morgan, *Images of Organization* (Beverly Hills: Sage, 1986).

6. Goldstein, *An Interview with Larry Hirschhorn,* op. cit., p. 18.

7. Peter Reid, *Well Made in America: Lessons From Harley-Davidson on Being the Best* (New York: McGraw-Hill, 1990).

CHAPTER 8

1. Gregory Bateson, *Steps to an Ecology of Mind* (New York: Ballantine Books, 1972). Bateson's concept of information has been extremely important in methods to bring about constructive change in that most crucial of all social systems—the family.

2. See, for example, Lynn Hoffman, *Foundations of Family Therapy: A Conceptual Framework for Systems* Change (New York: Basic Books, 1981).

3. "Difference questioning" is our term for what family systems therapists call "circular questions." See M. Selvini Palazzoli, L. Boscolo, G. Cecchin, and G. Prata, "Hypothesizing-Circularity-Neutrality," *Family Process* 19 (1): 73-85 (March 1980).The use of this difference question for generating far-from-equilibrium conditions was first described by the author of the present book in, "A Far-From-Equilibrium Approach to Resistance to Change," *Organizational Dynamics* 17 (2): 16-22 (1988).

4. This example is a modification from a similar one found in L. Boscolo, G. Cecchin, L. Hoffman, and P. Penn, *Milan Systemic Family Therapy* (New York: Basic Books, 1987), p. 33.

5. These ideas were first presented in Jeffrey Goldstein and Marjorie Leopold, "Equality and Difference: Resolving Intercultural Conflict," *Human Resource Horizons* 101 (Summer, 1990): 27-32.

CHAPTER 9

1. Margaret Wheatley, *Leadership and the New Science* (San Francisco: Berrett-Koehler Publishers, 1992). Meg Wheatley's work on information

overload is discussed in an interview with her conducted by the author: Jeffrey Goldstein, "Revisioning the Organization: Chaos, Quantum Physics, and OD," *Organization Development Journal* 11 (2): 85-91 (Summer 1993).

2. John Andrews, "Interpersonal Challenge: A Source of Growth in Laboratory Training," *Journal of Applied Behavioral Science* 9: 514-533 (1973).

3. This example comes from a conversation with Brenda Zimmerman of York University. She elaborates on her work with Fedmet in her doctoral dissertation, *Strategy, Chaos and Equilibrium: A Case Study of Federal Metals, Inc.* (York Univ., Canada, March, 1991).

4. This is similar to the process of structural tension between vision and current reality developed by Robert Fritz in *The Path of Least Resistance* (New York: Fawcett Columbine, 1989).

CHAPTER 10

1. M. Beer and E. Walton, "Developing the Competitive Organization: Interventions and Strategies," *The American Psychologist* 45 (1990): 154-161.

2. W. Gibb Dyer, Jr., "The Cycle of Cultural Evolution in Organizations," in *Gaining Control of the Corporate Culture*, ed. R. Kilmann, M. Saxton, R. Serpa (San Francisco: Jossey-Bass, 1985).

3. Y. Zeira and J. Avedisian, "Organizational Planned Change: Assessing the Chances for Success," *Organizational Dynamics* 17 (1989): 31-45. Actually, Zeira's and Avedisian's instrument is a type of Lewinian force-field analysis that we discussed in Chapter 2. It identifies forces that are progressive toward change, such as an internal champion, and forces that resist change, such as a nonsupportive organization culture. If the resisting forces predominate in the system, Zeira and Avedisian recommend that change agents turn their attention to changing the culture first. This tactic is an instance of Lewin's "unfreezing" of the "additional force field" of the organizational culture resisting change See also Jeffrey Goldstein, "Beyond Lewin's Force Field: A New Model for Organizational Change Interventions," F. Massarik, ed., *Advances in Organization Development*, volume 2 (Norwood, N.J.: Ablex Publishing Company, 1993), pp. 72-88.

Linda Ackerman suggested that change agents not only do an "impact analysis" of how the planned change will specifically affect functions, people, and management systems but they can also predict at what pace this change will proceed. This suggestion reveals a strong belief in predictability about the impact of a change intervention. See her article, "Transition Management: An In-depth Look at Managing Complex Change," *Organizational Dynamics* 11 (1982): 46-66.

4. See a discussion on the strange nonlinear behavior of one of the most simple nonlinear equations in Robert May, "Some Mathematical Models with Very Complicated Dynamics," *Nature* 261 (June 10, 1976): 459-467. See also Gregoire Nicolis and Ilya Prigogine, *Exploring Complexity* (New York: W.H. Freeman & Co., 1989), p. 14.

   This aspect of nonlinear unpredictability prompted computer scientist Ed Fredkin to remark: "There is no way to know the answer to some question [a nonlinear one] any faster than what's going on...[even God] cannot know the answer to the question any faster than doing it." (Quoted in R. Wright, *Three Scientists and Their Gods: Looking for Meaning in an Age of Information* (New York: Time Books, 1988), p. 68).

5. F. Westley, "The Eye of the Needle: Cultural and Personal Transformation in a Traditional Organization," *Human Relations* 43 (1990): 273-293.

6. Westley (1990), p. 286.

7. See the exploration of organizational noise in C. Ciborra, P. Migliarese, and P. Romano, "A Methodological Inquiry of Organizational Noise in Sociotechnical Systems," *Human Relations* 37 (8): 565-588 (1984).

8. See P. Allen and J. McGlade, "Evolutionary Drive: The Effect of Microscopic Diversity, Error Making and Noise," *Foundations of Physics* 17(7): 723-738 (1987). Nonaka, in his studies of successful Japanese corporations, has proposed that the creation of crises in these organizations facilitated innovative strategies to deal with the crises See I. Nonaka, "Creating Organizational Order out of Chaos: Self-renewal in Japanese Firms," *California Management Review* 30(3): 57-73 (1988). In this way crises can function as far-from-equilibrium conditions. However, why is it necessary to generate a crisis when chance events or random departures from equilibrium are taking place all the time in organizations? What is necessary, then, is not a crisis, but a way to take advantage of what is already taking place, i.e., the organizational noise.

9. Nicolis, "Physics of Far-from-equilibrium Systems and Self-organization," (see Chapter 3, note 1), p. 343.

10. James Austin, *Chase, Chance, and Creativity: The Lucky Art of Novelty* (New York: Columbia Univ. Press, 1978). See also Royston Roberts, *Serendipity: Accidental Discoveries in Science* (New York: John Wiley & Sons, 1989).

11. Austin, op. cit., p. 63.

12. Ibid., pp. 76, 77.

13. Dyer, "The Cycle of Cultural Evolution in Organizations," op. cit., p. 222.

14. This view of different possible outcomes and their unpredictable nature stands in marked contrast with the general systems approach to understanding organizational dynamics, in which the principle of equifinality has it that the organization will have many possible ways to reach a single goal (Ludwig von Bertalanffy, *Perspectives on General Systems Theory* (New York: George Braziller, 1975)). Such a viewpoint is actually an equilibrium-based model since it is claimed that this equifinality comes about from the restoration of equilibrium after a disturbance . Of course, in an equilibrium-seeking model, the final outcome is always predictable; it is the state of equilibrium. An isolated system will naturally tend to the state of equilibrium, even though the pathways taken to reach this final state are many and varied, and it may take some time for the transient phenomena that depart from equilibrium to die out. For equilibrium-based general systems models in organizational theory, see *General Systems and Organization Theory: Methodological Aspects*, ed. A. Melcher (Kent, Ohio: Kent State Univ. Press, 1975).

15. Carl Whitaker, "Psychotherapy of the Absurd: With a Special Emphasis on the Psychotherapy of Aggression," *Family Process* 14 (1): 1-16 (March 1975). This work with the absurd is similar to the practices of the late psychiatrist Milton Erickson: confusing the system to depotentiate limited mindsets or normal belief systems. See Milton Erickson and Ernest Rossi, *Hypnotherapy: An Exploratory Casebook* (New York: Irvington Publishers, 1979).

16. Richard Nodell and Eric Wolff, *Managerial Magic: A Medicine Man's Guide to Organizational Life* (Dubuque, Iowa: Kendall/Hunt Publishing, 1989).

17. Nan Kilkeary, *The Good Communicator* (Evanston, Illinois: Quik Read, 1987).

ABOUT THE AUTHOR

Jeffrey Goldstein, Ph.D., has been a full-time faculty member in the Department of Administrative Sciences, Schools of Business, Adelphi University, Garden City, NY since 1989. Professor Goldstein has also taught at Rutgers University, Columbia University, NYU, and Temple University. As a consultant to many public and private businesses and institutions, Dr. Goldstein has been primarily interested in how to help organizations bring about deep-rooted change.

Professor Goldstein has published over 30 articles and is a frequent presenter at professional conferences. For the past seven years, his primary focus of research has been the application of the new nonlinear systems sciences to the study of organizational dynamics. This has included research and writing on chaos theory, far-from-equilibrium thermodynamics, complex, adaptive systems theory, and nonlinear dynamical systems theory. Dr. Goldstein is a member of the Society for Chaos Theory in Psychology and the Life Sciences, the Chaos Network, and Chaos in Praxis.

INDEX

BOOKS FROM PRODUCTIVITY PRESS

Productivity Press provides individuals and companies with materials they need to achieve excellence in quality, productivity and the creative involvement of all employees. Through sets of learning tools and techniques, Productivity supports continuous improvement as a vision, and as a strategy. Many of our leading-edge products are direct source materials translated into English for the first time from industrial leaders around the world. Call toll-free 1-800-394-6868 for our free catalog.

Modeling for Learning Organizations
John Morecroft and John Sterman, eds.

An outstanding compilation of articles by top system dynamics thinkers worldwide, offering a "user-friendly" introduction to leading edge methods of organization modeling and answers to many of the questions raised by Peter Senge's best-selling book *The Fifth Discipline*. Part 1 discusses generally how modeling can support management decision making. Parts 2 and 3 offer case studies. Part 4 evaluates the latest software technology for computer simulation modeling.
ISBN 1-56327-060-9 / 426 pages / price $45.00 / Order XMLO-B117

Introduction to Computer Simulation
Nancy Roberts, David Andersen, Ralph Deal, Michael Garet, William Shaffer

Simulation as an aid to solving problems has been a powerful tool for centuries. With the advent of the computer revolution, this tool has come within the reach of virtually everyone. This book is both an introduction to systems thinking—the critical element in problem solving for complex organizations—and a "how to" on building computer simulation models. Primarily developed as a classroom text, it is also a perfect vehicle for professionals in many different arenas (including business, government, and the social sciences) who want to reshape their organizations and their products or services by using system dynamics to solve complex problems. It provides a practical, concrete method for using computer simulation to model complex systems. No computer experience is required.
ISBN 1-56327-052-8 / 570 pages / $35.00 / Order XICS-B117

Companywide Quality Management
Alberto Galgano

Companywide quality management (CWQM) leads to dramatic changes in management values and priorities, company culture, management of company operations, management and decision-making processes, techniques and methods used by employees, and more. Much has been written on this subject, but Galgano—a leading European consultant who studied with leaders of the Japanese quality movement—offers hands-on, stage-front knowledge of the monumental changes CWQC can bring.
ISBN 1-56327-038-2 / 480 pages / $45.00 / Order CWQM-B117

Productivity Press, Inc., Dept. BK, P.O. Box 13390, Portland, OR 97213-0390
Telephone: 1-800-394-6868   Fax: 1-800-394-6286

Feedback Toolkit
16 Tools for Better Communication in the Workplace
Rick Maurer

In companies striving to reduce hierarchy and foster trust and responsible participation, good person-to-person feedback can be as important as sophisticated computer technology in enabling effective teamwork. Feedback is an important map of your situation, a way to tell whether you are "on or off track." Used well, feedback can motivate people to their highest level of performance. Despite its significance, this level of information sharing makes most managers uncomfortable. *Feedback Toolkit* addresses this natural hesitation with an easy-to-grasp 6-step framework and 16 practical and creative approaches for giving and receiving feedback with individuals and groups. Maurer's reality-tested methods in *Feedback Toolkit* are indispensable equipment for managers and teams in every organization.
ISBN 1-56327-056-0 / 109 pages / $15.00 / Order FEED-B117

Caught in the Middle
A Leadership Guide for Partnership in the Workplace
Rick Maurer

Managers today are caught between old skills and new expectations. You're expected not only to improve quality and services, but also to get staff more involved. This stimulating book provides the inspiration and know-how to achieve these goals as it brings to light the rewards of establishing a real partnership with your staff. Includes self-assessment questionnaires.
ISBN 1-56327-004-8 / 258 pages / $30.00 / Order CAUGHT-B117

Corporate Planning and Policy Design
A System Dynamics Approach (3rd ed.)
James M. Lyneis

System dynamics is a tool for planning and policy design that provides insight into the many critical problem areas in growing companies, including under-performance, production and inventory instability, improving response to growth, product shortages, labor instability, lost market share, adverse consequences of financial control of inventory, and excess capacity. See how this remarkable tool for corporate planning can work for your organization.
ISBN 0-262-12083-6 / 520 pages / $45.00 / Order XCPPD-B117

Handbook for Personal Productivity
Henry E. Liebling

A little book with a lot of power that will help you become more successful and satisfied at work, as well as in your personal life. This pocket-sized handbook offers sections on personal productivity improvement, team achievement, quality customer service, improving your health, and how to get the most out of workshops and seminars. Special bulk discounts are available (call for more information).
ISBN 0-915299-94-1 / 128 pages / $9.00 paper / Order PP-B117

PRODUCTIVITY PRESS, INC., DEPT. BK, P.O. BOX 13390, PORTLAND, OR 97213-0390
Telephone: 1-800-394-6868   Fax: 1-800-394-6286

Fast Focus on TQM
A Concise Guide to Companywide Learning
Derm Barrett

Finally, here's one source for all your TQM questions. Compiled in this concise, easy-to-read handbook are definitions and detailed explanations of over 300 key terms used in TQM. Organized in a simple alphabetical glossary form, the book can be used either as a primer for anyone being introduced to TQM or as a complete reference guide. It helps to align teams, departments, or entire organizations in a common understanding and use of TQM terminology. For anyone entering or currently involved in TQM, this is one resource you must have.
ISBN 1-56327-049-8 / approx. 200 pages / $20.00 / Order FAST-B117

Handbook for Productivity Measurement and Improvement
William F. Christopher and Carl G. Thor, eds.

An unparalleled resource! In over 100 chapters, nearly 80 front-runners in the quality movement reveal the evolving theory and specific practices of world-class organizations. Spanning a wide variety of industries and business sectors, they discuss quality and productivity in manufacturing, service industries, profit centers, administration, nonprofit and government institutions, health care and education. Contributors include Robert C. Camp, Peter F. Drucker, Jay W. Forrester, Joseph M. Juran, Robert S. Kaplan, John W. Kendrick, Yasuhiro Monden, and Lester C. Thurow. Comprehensive in scope and organized for easy reference, this compendium belongs in every company and academic institution concerned with business and industrial viability.
ISBN 1-56327-007-2 / 1344 pages / $90.00 / Order HPM-B117

Hoshin Kanri
Policy Deployment for Successful TQM
Yoji Akao (ed.)

Hoshin kanri, the Japanese term for policy deployment, is an approach to strategic planning and quality improvement that has become a pillar of Total Quality Management (TQM) for a growing number of U.S. firms. This book is a compilation of examples of policy deployment that demonstrates how company vision is converted into individual responsibility. It includes practical guidelines, 150 charts and diagrams, and five case studies that illustrate the procedures of hoshin kanri. The six steps to advanced process planning are reviewed and include a five-year vision, one-year plan, deployment to departments, execution, monthly audit, and annual audit.
ISBN 0-915299-57-7 / 241 pages / $65.00 / Order HOSHIN-B117

PRODUCTIVITY PRESS, INC., DEPT. BK, P.O. BOX 13390, PORTLAND, OR 97213-0390
Telephone: 1-800-394-6868   Fax: 1-800-394-6286

The Hunters and the Hunted
A Non-Linear Solution for Reengineering the Workplace
James B. Swartz

Because our competitive environment changes so rapidly—weekly, even daily—if you want to survive, you have to stay on top of those changes. Otherwise, you become prey to your competitors. Hunters continuously change and learn; anyone who doesn't becomes the hunted and sooner or later will be devoured. This unusual non-fiction novel provides a veritable crash course in continuous transformation. It offers lessons from real-life companies and introduces many industrial gurus as characters, as well providing a riveting story of two strong people struggling to turn their company around. *The Hunters and the Hunted* doesn't simply tell you how to change; it puts you inside the change process itself.
ISBN 1-56327-043-9 / 582 pages / $45.00 / Order HUNT-B117

A New American TQM
Four Practical Revolutions in Management
Shoji Shiba, Alan Graham, and David Walden

For TQM to succeed in America, you need to create an American-style "learning organization" with the full commitment and understanding of senior managers and executives. Written expressly for this audience, *A New American TQM* offers a comprehensive and detailed explanation of TQM and how to implement it, based on courses taught at MIT's Sloan School of Management and the Center for Quality Management, a consortium of American hi-tech companies. Full of case studies and amply illustrated, the book examines major quality tools and how they are being used by the most progressive American companies today.
ISBN 1-56327-032-3 / 606 pages / $50.00 / Order NATQM-B117

The New Standardization
Keystone of Continuous Improvement in Manufacturing
Shigehiro Nakamura

In an era of continuous improvement and ISO 9000, quality is not an option but a requirement—and you can't set or meet criteria for quality without standardization. Standardization lets you share information about the best ways to do things so that they will be done that way consistently. This book shows how to make standardization a living system of just-in-time information that delivers exactly the information that's needed, exactly when it is needed, and exactly where it is needed. It's the only way to sustain the results of your improvement efforts in every area of your company.
ISBN 1-56327-039-0 / 286 pages / $75.00 / Order STAND-B117

PRODUCTIVITY PRESS, INC., DEPT. BK, P.O. BOX 13390, PORTLAND, OR 97213-0390
Telephone: 1-800-394-6868   Fax: 1-800-394-6286

The Idea Book
Improvement Through TEI (Total Employee Involvement)
Japan Human Relations Association

At last, a book showing how to create Total Employee Involvement (TEI) and get hundreds of ideas from each employee every year to improve every aspect of your organization. Gathering improvement ideas from your entire workforce is a must for global competitiveness. *The Idea Book,* heavily illustrated, is a hands-on teaching tool for workers and supervisors to refer to again and again. Perfect for study groups, too.
ISBN 0-915299-22-4 / 232 pages / $55.00 / Order IDEA-B117

Individual Motivation
Removing the Blocks to Creative Involvement
Etienne Minarik

The key to gaining the competitive advantage in a saturated market is to use existing resources more efficiently and creatively. This book shows managers how to turn employees' "negative individualism" into creativity and initiative. It describes the shift in corporate culture necessary to enable front-line employees to use their knowledge about product and process to the company's greatest benefit.
ISBN 0-915299-85-2 / 263 pages / $30.00 / Order INDM-B117

Industrial Dynamics
Jay W. Forrester

Industrial Dynamics is an experimental, quantitative philosophy for designing corporate structures and policies that are compatible with an organization's growth and stability objectives. From analysis of organization structure and complex internal interactions, Forrester offers insight into the influence of management actions on the dynamic characteristics of an organization. For managers and students of managerial science.
ISBN 0-915299-88-7 / 464 pages / $50.00 paper / Order XINDDY-B117

Measuring, Managing, and Maximizing Performance
Will Kaydos

You do not need to be an exceptionally skilled technician or inspirational leader to improve your company's quality and productivity. In non-technical, jargon-free, practical terms this book details the entire process of improving performance, from why and how the improvement process work to what must be done to begin and to sustain continuous improvement of performance. Special emphasis is given to the role that performance measurement plays in identifying problems and opportunities.
ISBN 0-915299-98-4 / 284 pages / $40.00 / Order MMMP-B117

PRODUCTIVITY PRESS, INC., DEPT. BK, P.O. BOX 13390, PORTLAND, OR 97213-0390
Telephone: 1-800-394-6868   Fax: 1-800-394-6286

Principles of Systems

Jay W. Forrester

The basic introductory text on system dynamics philosophy and method-ology. It introduces the basic concepts of system structure, then shows by example how structure determines behavior. Although the problems are framed in a corporate context, the principles are general to many fields. Due to the general nature of the principles discussed, the book is suitable for teaching courses on dynamics of urban, ecological, corporate, and other complex systems. It can be used either for self study or as a class textbook.
ISBN 0-915299-87-9 / 392 pages / $25.00 paper / Order XPRSYS-B117

The Teamwork Advantage
An Inside Look at Japanese Product and Technology Development
Jeffrey L. Funk

How are so many Japanese manufacturing firms shortening product time-to-market, reducing costs, and improving quality? The answer is teamwork. Dr. Funk spent 18 months as a visiting engineer at Mitsubishi and Yokogawa Hokushin Electric and knows firsthand how Japanese corporate culture promotes effective teamwork in production, design, and technology develop-ment. Here's a penetrating case study and analysis that presents a truly viable model for the West.
ISBN 0-915299-69-0 / 508 pages / $50.00 / Order TEAMAD-B117

Vision Management
Translating Strategy into Action
SANNO Management Development Research Center (ed.)

For over ten years, managers of Japan's top companies have gathered at SANNO University to brainstorm about innovative corporate management methods. This book is based on the proven methodology that evolved from their ideas. It describes how the intangible aspects of vision-based strategy can be integrated into a concrete implementation model and clarifies the rela-tionship among vision, strategy, objectives, goals, and day-to-day activities.
ISBN 0-915299-80-1 / 272 pages / $30.00 / Order VISM-B117

Cycle Time Management
The Fast Track to Time-Based Productivity Improvement
Patrick Northey and Nigel Southway

As much as 90 percent of the operational activities in a traditional plant are nonessential or pure waste. This book presents a proven methodology for elimi-nating this waste within 24 to 30 months by measuring productivity in terms of time instead of revenue or people. CTM is a cohesive management strategy that integrates just-in-time (JIT) production, computer integrated manufacturing (CIM), and total quality control (TQC). From this succinct, highly-focused book, you'll learn what CTM is, how to implement it, and how to manage it.
ISBN 1-56327-015-3 / 200 pages / $35.00 / Order CYCLE-B117

PRODUCTIVITY PRESS, INC., DEPT. BK, P.O. BOX 13390, PORTLAND, OR 97213-0390
Telephone: 1-800-394-6868   Fax: 1-800-394-6286

TO ORDER: Write, phone, or fax Productivity Press, Dept. BK, 541 NE 20th Ave., Portland, OR 97232, phone 1-800-394-6868, fax 1-800-394-6286. Send check or charge to your credit card (American Express, Visa, MasterCard accepted).

U.S. ORDERS: Add $5 shipping for first book, $2 each additional for UPS surface delivery. We offer attractive quantity discounts for bulk purchases of individual titles; call for more information.

INTERNATIONAL ORDERS: Write, phone, or fax for quote and indicate shipping method desired. For international callers, telephone number is 503-235-0600 and fax number is 503-235-0909. Prepayment in U.S. dollars must accompany your order (checks must be drawn on U.S. banks). When quote is returned with payment, your order will be shipped promptly by the method requested.

NOTE: Prices are in U.S. dollars and are subject to change without notice.